the Idler book of

CRAP TOWNS II

THE NATION DECIDES

THE NEW TOP 50 WORST PLACES TO LIVE IN THE UK

Edited by Sam Jordison and Dan Kieran

B■XTREE

MORE COMMENTS ON THE
FIRST BOOK OF CRAP TOWNS

'Magnificent.' *Guardian*

'A tasteless joke.' *Western Daily Press*

'Great book! But Glasgow is missing.' *Dauvit Alexander*

'Here we go again, yet another book devoted to how dreadful Britain is, how very original! Yes all UK cities are crap really, aren't they? In fact I think I'll go and live in Norilsk in Russia because you know British cities are absolutely awful. Lagos knocks spots of Manchester doesn't it? What a load of garbage.' *James*

'Fucking bunch off wankers, the lot of you.' *CCSC*

First published 2004 by Boxtree an imprint of Pan Macmillan Ltd
Pan Macmillan, 20 New Wharf Road, London N1 9RR
Basingstoke and Oxford
Associated companies throughout the world
www.panmacmillan.com

ISBN 0 7522 2545 6

9 8 7 6 5 4 3 2 1

A CIP catalogue record for this book is available from the British Library

Typeset by Liz Harris
Printed by Bath Press

Edited by
Sam Jordison and Dan Kieran

Designed by Liz Harris

Illustrations by Gwyn

Front cover photograph by Lorna Hughes

CONTENTS

▼ ■
KEY: symbols show position in first book

BRITAIN IS STILL CRAP.

If the publication of the first book of *Crap Towns* proved anything, it was that there's an unlimited supply of undesirable locations in the UK.

It was a huge success and, we're happy to say, in spite of a few understandably aggrieved local burghers and conservative worthies, most people found it quite funny.

There was, however, a problem.

'Why the hell isn't Luton in there?'

We were asked this again and again, with subtle variations on the theme involving Milton Keynes, Port Talbot, Sunderland and Windsor.

We couldn't answer.

It was clear there was still an awful lot of work to be done. There were rich veins of high-grade crap all over the nation, just waiting to be mined.

Computers at Crap Towns' headquarters seized up under the strain, it took hours to even get into the email inbox and longer still to make any sense of the crazed missives it contained. Eventually, spitting and hissing all the way, the machines dredged up a list of 100 likely candidates for the title of Britain's worst town. Some were old; more were new. All, we were told, were awful.

The list was published in newspapers across the land and the discussion was opened up to the public. After much heated debate, more mad email correspondence and the pronouncements of several top politicians, the nation decided on the final 50.

You hold the results in your hands.

And no, we don't know why Watford didn't make it either. Maybe next time.

50 CHESTER

Antiqui colant antiquum dierum
(Let the ancients worship
the ancient of days)

Population: **118,000**
Unemployment: **2.4%**
Violent crimes: **8**
(per 1,000 per annum)
% achieving 5 or more
GCSE grades A-C: **69**

Famous residents: **Russ Abbot, Giles Brandreth**

James Boswell told Samuel Johnson that: 'Chester pleases me more than any town I ever saw.' Sadly, although the town cultivates an image of reverend antiquity, things have changed greatly since the self-confessed whore-obsessed biographer wrote those words in 1779.

Chester is classed as a city because it has its own cathedral. However, this 'impressive' edifice is actually the size of your average village church, and has turned a lovely shade of black due to the amount of filth that comes out of the mouths of the locals.

Noted as a tourist attraction, you can choose between walking the fabulous Roman walls (largely rebuilt this century), the authentic half-timbered town centre (Victorians faking ye olde medieval times), or the famous Chester rows (an excuse to fit in twice as many shops as is decent).

Local hobbies include shoplifting, smack-taking al fresco, hippy/tramp beating and seeing how many times one can fit 'mate-o' into any normal conversation.

Don't be fooled by the glamour of *Hollyoaks*, which is largely filmed in Liverpool now because Chester's local scallies gave the cast and crew too much shit.

CHARLOTTE COOPER

BAD SEX

On a sunny day it's a pretty enough town, but not as flash as it likes to think it is. The locals talk with Southern accents and look down their noses at the people from Blacon, North Wales and the Wirral, who all pile in to get bladdered at its bars and urinate in its streets.

All the lasses come from miles around in their high heels and little satin dresses, dripping

CRAP TOWN TRIVIA Jonathan Swift regularly passed through Chester on his journey to and from Ireland. He wrote:

The walls of this town
Are full of renown,
And strangers delight to walk round 'em;
But as for the dwellers,
Both buyers and sellers,
For me, you may hang 'em or drown 'em.

THE VIEW FROM
CHESTER'S FAMOUS
CITY WALLS

jewellery, to find their Cheshire millionaires. All the lads strut around in their work suits pretending to be those Cheshire millionaires. Then they all go home and have angry, bad, unsatisfying sex, dreaming of football stars, Ferraris, high-rolling trips to Monaco and *Hollyoaks* actresses.

NICK LACEY

MISERABLE FUNNY MAN

My home town is the only place where I've been started on by a bunch of girls, for not looking at them. I also fondly recall a night, a few years ago, where two of my mates were beaten up by a troop of silverback bouncers from the legendary Joe's Wine Bar for standing next to a car belonging to one of said apes. No-one of note has ever come from Chester, apart from Russ Abbot – and when I spotted him in the Grosvenor Precinct he was frowning.

ANDREW MORRIS

IN DEFENCE OF CHESTER

Every town gets lumbered with its handful of mouthy moaners, but a city with six million visitors a year, which is still going strong after 2000 years, must be getting something right.

Perhaps it is our heritage after all. The most complete walled city in Britain, with a

Roman amphitheatre, fascinating ancient streets, a stunning red sandstone medieval cathedral, the oldest racecourse in Britain set on the beautiful banks of River Dee… the list is endless.

Or is it that our historic shopping centre, the Rows, has helped place Chester, with a population of 120,000, at the number 11 spot of top shopping destinations in the whole of the United Kingdom?

Then again it could be the vibrant café and restaurant culture, which attracts people from all over the NorthWest and beyond.

As for Russ Abbot frowning, I can only imagine that he must have bumped into a few of your miserable contributors. They should get out more!

PAUL CHADWICK

SENIOR PARLIAMENTARY RESEARCHER TO CHRISTINE RUSSELL, MP, MEMBER OF PARLIAMENT FOR THE CITY OF CHESTER

BUILD YOUR CRAP TOWN LEXICON

Scally (n) – *a bad lad from the North West who steals things, starts fights and makes odd hand gestures that generally involve pointing at the floor. cf Ned*
Chavs (n) – *wide-boys or girls who dress so expensively and tastelessly that they look like they come from Chatham.*
Orcs (n) *1. Evil creatures under the control of the Dark Lord Sauron.*
2. Kids who sniff glue and shout abuse at pedestrians.

49 CLEATOR MOOR

Population: **7,000**
Unemployment: **5%**
Violent crimes: **8**
(per 1,000 per annum)
% achieving 5 or more
GCSE grades A-C: **n/a**
Famous residents: **L.S.**
Lowry did a picture of a church

Cleator Moor lies in beautiful countryside close to the Georgian splendours of Whitehaven. Full of old buildings and mercifully free of traffic, it would be quite attractive if years of neglect and lack of investment hadn't left it rotting.

This wild west Cumbrian town is a forgotten outcrop on a forgotten part of England, neglected since the Great Depression destroyed it almost 100 years ago. It most closely resembles the town in *Pale Rider* – after Clint Eastwood has killed nearly everyone, painted the houses red and renamed it Hell.

There is one long, infinitely desolate main street full of dangerous pubs, smashed-up cars and heavily fortified shops. The few bored inhabitants drift around like tumbleweeds, looking for someone like you to hit. They're so hard that when they die they are used to hold up bridges. When they're alive they're more dangerous than sarin gas. And they have generations of anger to expound, rightfully pissed off at the way no one has ever done anything to help them or their unhappy homes.

The closest 'outsiders' ever get to Cleator Moor is when they tramp within a mile of its boundaries on Wainwright's Coast to Coast walk. The famously straight-talking creator of the cross-country trek advised anyone thinking of taking a diversion into the town to 'abandon hope'.

BILLY BADMATCHES

PHOTOS: DAN KIERAN (LEFT); SAM JORDISON (RIGHT)

48 BELFAST

Pro tanto quid retrebamus
(What shall we give in return for so much)

Population: **277,391**
Unemployment: **4%**
Famous residents:
Alex 'Hurricane' Higgins, George Best

The tanks are now gone, the barriers are down and hopefully the worst of The Troubles in Belfast are over. But the bad memories linger, on while the bad weather is a source of derisive amusement even for Mancunians.

The warped gothic architecture of Belfast is overwhelming and magnificent – but that's the only tangible benefit of living in a religiously confused backwater.

Life was worse in the 1970s and 1980s when psychos roamed the grey terraced streets on a crusade of violence, inspired by religious views that would frighten the average Taliban Mullah, but even now if you walk five minutes from the (admittedly fine) new pubs in the city centre, you enter a nightmare world of almost medieval extremes.

There is a certain dark humour to be found from the absurdity of living in a city where the biggest political party spent most of the 1980s trying to save us from 'Frankie Goes To Hollywood' but that doesn't really compensate for the horrors of religious bigotry, grinding poverty, random sectarian violence and dreadful traditional Irish music.

MD

47 CARDIFF
Europe's youngest capital

Population: **305,000**
Unemployment: **3.1%**
Violent crimes: **13.1**
(per 1,000 per
annum)
Famous residents:
**Shirley Bassey, Howard Jones,
Charlotte Church, Tom Jones**

*Cardiff is undergoing something
of a renaissance, with the arrival
of the Welsh Assembly and the
finest stadium in the UK. Not
enough of a renaissance for
many, however.*

It claims to be a capital city but
really it's small, partisan and
insular.

There is nothing to do in
Cardiff. Nothing. Except maybe
take a sightseeing bus around
the government buildings and
Cardiff Bay … taking all of five
minutes out of your day. This
bay consists of a prefab hut
where the Welsh Assembly
meets. There is also a cinema/restaurant complex
where you can fight off boredom for about two
hours before its sickly, modern synthetic nature
becomes all too much. Then you're just left with
miles and miles of derelict land …
NICK JACOBSEN

CARDIFF CULTURE
There is no doubt that Cardiff is the cultural
mecca of South Wales. Imagine a gold rush town
from an old Western - a shimmering oasis filled
with people on the make, ready to fight at the
drop of a bottle Bacardi Breezer, and surrounded
by tumble weeded wilderness. Apparently having
more shops than any other town in a hundred
mile radius makes a capital out of a pretty
ordinary city.

CRAP TOWN TRIVIA Cardiff became a capital city in 1955. Bratislava became a capital city (of Slovakia) in 1993. From this, it is possible to deduce that Cardiff is not – as its motto claims – Europe's youngest capital.

Gets you to the heart of Cardiff

For information on train times and fares visit www.valleylines.co.uk   Valley Lines

Which explains why when you visit Cardiff on a Saturday afternoon you'll see lots of bemused valley people wandering round and round the St David's shopping centre, looking for Peacocks but finding Oasis, marvelling at the fact that you can shop indoors and wondering whether they'll ever be as glamorous as the girls in Debenhams.

Sadly even the call of a Fruit of the Loom jumper and a Benetton drawstring rucksack couldn't keep me in South Wales for long - the worry that I'd end up married to someone named Bryn and spawn a child called Geraint was too much.

Now I live in South London where I'll probably have a child called Lemar.

NATALIE

IN DEFENCE OF CARDIFF

It sounds to me like Nick Jacobsen was beaten senseless by some drunken Cardiffian he offended on his last visit, and obviously has totally missed the point about Cardiff if his idea of a good time is sitting on a bus.

For anyone who has seen the likes of *Human Traffic*, or is into a seriously good time, then Cardiff is the place for you. We have one of the top ice hockey teams in the country, The Devils, and the rugby team, is awesome too. It's the home of the Millennium Stadium, and we hosted the Rugby World Cup in 1999.

Cardiff has been voted the fastest growing city in Europe for the past three years. Not bad for a crap town.

DARREN EVANS

SERIOUS AS CANCER

In response to Darren Evans' defence ('fastest growing city in Europe for the past three years'), as a resident of the city, I am drawn to point out that certain forms of malignant tumour are among the fastest growing of organic structures.

RICHARD JOHN EVANS

WELSH BY NAME?
WELSH FAMILY TARTANS

JONES
DAVIES
EVANS
HUGHES
MORGAN
HOPKINS
RHYS
PROBERT
OWEN
POWELL
MORRIS
LLOYD
WYNN
MEREDITH
VAUGHAN
PROTHEROE
CRADDOCK
PRITCHARD
TUDOR
RICE
CECIL

MERLIN
PENROSE
YORATH
PREECE
YALE
DEE
MADOC
PUGH
RICHARD
CONWAY
ARTHUR
LLEWELLYN
GLYN
HOWELLS
JENKINS
PRICE
GRIFFITHS
LEWIS
ROBERTS
THOMAS
WILLIAMS

46 GRAVESEND

Population: **96,000**
Unemployment: **3.5**
Violent crimes: **8.2**
(per 1,000 per annum)
Famous residents:
Mickey from *The Bill*, Herr Flick from *'Allo 'Allo*

Gravesend was once the last sight many sailors saw before leaving England. Which helps explain why our empire was so far flung.

CRAP TOWN TRIVIA
There was at least some excitement at Gravesend on election nights in the nineteenth century. Each political party hauled a burning boat around the town and, when they met, mass brawls would break out between their supporters. The tradition went on until 1870 when the police finally put a stop to it.

In most nations and cultures it is deemed desirable to live by a river, with tranquil flowing waters, riverside walks and memorable vistas. But then there's Gravesend, where the tea-brown waters rush past carrying the detritus from local factories, the riverside walks are marred by dog-poo strewn pavements, and the only views are of the Tilbury docks on the Essex shore.

With most of the oldest buildings destroyed in a series of fires in the town centre during the eighteenth and nineteenth centuries, the current buildings are a far cry from the era during the reign of Queen Victoria when the town was a resort for tourists from London.

Londoners now avoid Gravesend like the plague, but there are a few American Disney enthusiasts who've been coming to the town to view the burial grounds of Pocahontas, the ill-fated Indian princess immortalised in the animated movie.

According to legend, she lost the will to live on reaching Gravesend (understandably enough), and died in March 1617. A statue in the grounds of St George's Church, tucked away round the back of the shopping centre car park, marks her visit to the town.

There was a dig to unearth the princess's remains in 1923. Nothing was found.

The tourists usually leave soon after they've seen the statue, looking bemused (and more than a little scared), no doubt

wondering whether their trip was even worth the train fare, for there is absolutely nothing else for them to do in Gravesend.

But what else can you expect? Let's face it, the name says it all.

ANDREW

45 LEEDS
Pro lege et rege
(For the king and the law)

Population: **715,000**
Unemployment: **3.3%**
Violent crimes: **8 (per 1,000 per annum)**
% achieving 5 or more GCSE grades A-C: **69**
Famous residents: **David Gedge, 'The Sisters of Mercy', Jimmy Savile**

Leeds has overcome years of industrial decline to become a bold, brash shopping centre full of bright lights, theme pubs and out-of-control drunkards.

City of random shouting and violence. The epitome of which is probably the local football team and the allegations about its racist thugs.

Go to any city at 2 a.m. and you'll see drunken people stumbling about and shouting, perhaps engaging in mindless violence. Go to Leeds and you'll see all this and more, 24 hours a day.

Add to this the hopeless transport infrastructure – trains are often late and cancelled because of the track in disrepair and/or the half-finished station (which has been under re-development for aeons). Wait for hours at a bus stop and you might be lucky enough for a nearly empty bus to pull up, let people off and then refuse to let anyone else get on.

Yes, Leeds, 'the London of the North' – if you're going on the number of homeless people wandering its streets, perhaps.

MARK SHEPHARD

TRADITIONAL LEEDS

On first impression you might believe Leeds to be something of a trendy oasis in the desert of abrasive lad culture that is the North of England. You'd be wrong. Despite the whole-hearted embracing of the new 'trendy' mullet-effect hairstyle and attendant camp clothing there is no erosion of the aggressive, parochial mentality that has traditionally characterised inhabitants of Leeds.

Nights out consist of protracted bouts of posturing and preening, but with no reduction in the chance of your getting a good 'shoeing' for the slightest offence. The good people of Leeds seem to take great pride in the fact that the city centre is horrendously over-priced, despite the fact that you can get the same bland cocktail of fun pubs and mutton dressed as

Conde Nast Traveller magazine recently dubbed Leeds 'The UK's favourite city'. *Lonely Planet* calls it the 'Knightsbridge of the North'. Leeds is the most popular university choice in the country and the fastest growing city. It also holds the country's worst record for animal cruelty.

lamb for half the cost in any of the surrounding towns.

PAUL

WELL-MANNERED MUGGERS

An injustice has been done to Leeds. Since when was a town judged solely on the behaviour of two members of its football team? I lived in Leeds for 18 years and was only the subject of

violence once. It was in the bowling alley. A 12-year-old with a flick knife 'borrowed a pound off me'. He was quite polite for a mugger, although he hadn't yet reached puberty.

People may confuse the vocal harshness of the Leeds Yorkshire accent (a far cry from the James Herriot style North Yorkshire burr) with an undertone of a threat of violence. They are wrong to do so – if they can manage to understand what a Leodensian is saying, they would do well to talk to him – there are few more friendly or funnier people, always willing to just stop and pass the time of day.

The club doormen are friendly, too. I even saw one ejecting a client from a bar with the offer of a pint on the house next time he was in.

OLIVER ISAACS

A BARROVIAN WRITES

Maybe I'm biased because of my roots (I come from Barrow-in-Furness) but I like Leeds! There's electricity and Channel 5!

ROBERT MOORE

44 THORPENESS

Population: **200**
Violent crimes: **6.5 (per 1,000 per annum)**

More of a golf club than a town, Thorpeness represents the apotheosis of middle England snobbery. Sure, the mock-Tudor thatched mansions are attractive, but no amount of twee flower arranging will hide the darkness of the inhabitants' souls.

'Don't even think of parking here', yell the signs. 'Private. Members only'. 'Access for RESIDENTS ONLY'. 'Polite notice. If you can't afford to live here, fuck off.'

SAMUEL DAVIDS

PHOTO: SAM JORDISON

43 BOURNEMOUTH

Pulchritudo et salubritas
(Beauty and debauchery)

Population: **163,000**
Unemployment: **3%**
Violent crimes: **9 (per 1,000 per annum)**
% achieving 5 or more GCSE grades A-C: **69**

Famous residents: **Alan Davey of 'Hawkwind', Sir Richard Attenborough, Max Bygraves, Alex from 'Blur', Drummy Zwebb from 'Aswad'**

*Tuscany, Bermuda, The Pyrenees…
Tony Blair may be a war-hungry scumbag, but there'd be no doubting his good taste in holiday destinations if only he weren't so keen on holding conferences in Bournemouth.*

With its very ordinary shopping precinct, very hostile clubs, very own Eye (a tethered balloon), love of traffic, endless hotels, depressing labyrinthian suburbs and determination to rid itself of any echoes of the past, Bournemouth will soon have earned the right to call itself the symbol of modern Britain.

That's why Tony Blair likes to go there for conferences. That's why the prestigious Bournemouth Symphony Orchestra is almost bankrupt. That's why we hope the sea level will rise and wash it all away.

CHRIS YATES

WALLY POLY

'But Bournemouth has a university – a venerable seat of learning …' Indeed. Until recently, however, Bournemouth University, based at Wallisdown, was known to all and sundry as 'Wally Poly'. You see, far from being impressed by troublesome qualifications, Bournemouthians gauge success in terms of horsepower or how many headlights you can fit on your Fiesta.

MARK BAKER

PHOTO: SAM JORDISON

42 HEMEL HEMPSTEAD

Population: **80,000**
Famous residents:
**Vinnie Jones used
to live nearby,
David Vanian from
'The Damned', Goldie**

*Hemel is best known for its daft
roundabout systems: and most
people outside its confines
haven't even heard of them.*

Most, nay all, new towns are
grim, but try imagining one
strategically placed between
Milton Keynes and Watford.
   There's no centre to the town
(apart from a strip of mostly
empty shops in a shopping
centre called The Marlows);
very few pubs (Hello? How is
this going to work?), and a
violent culture born of boredom
and unemployment. I rest my
case with this quote from the
best local website, hemelweb:

PHOTOS: SAM JORDISON

YUPPIE PARADISE

With a fantastic pretension to grandeur, Manchester has reinvented itself as a steel, chrome and glass yuppie paradise.

Every scrap of land and every beat-up warehouse seems to have been turned into a block of hastily constructed flats.

And, of course, it looks better.

A city pumped full of steel and chrome is going to look grand. On the other hand, the flimsy blocks built for the BMW-driving yahoos make whole areas of the city look like Benidorm during the package-holiday boom. The same breeze blocks, the same tiny balconies, the same back-to-backs huddled along the grubby city centre canal.

'the most famous landmark probably being the "magic" roundabout, which in fact is a series of small roundabouts around one big one'.

KATHYRN SAVILLE

CHEAP, BUT NOT CHEERFUL

Hemel Hempstead was designed with all the humanity and warmth of a travel lodge economy room.

ANDY PATE

ROVING REPORTER'S VERDICT

I was diverted through Hemel Hempstead on a coach, thanks to rail repair work in the Milton Keynes area. When it drove past three local suedeheads, they took out their manhoods and started beating them vigorously to the surprised consternation of most of the passengers, except an old man to my left, who just said: 'Typical bloody Hemel that'. **SJ**

PEACEHAVEN

SOUTH COAST
GLAZING
PEACEHAVEN

GLASS CUT TO SIZE
& GLAZING SERVICE

PEACEHAVEN
TWINNED WITH
EPINAY-SOUS-SENART
AND ISERNHAGEN

41 PEACEHAVEN

Population: 3,000
Famous residents:
Gracie Fields

In Graham Greene's *Brighton Rock* the criminal anti-hero Pinkie takes his tragic lover Rose to the outskirts of this ironically named town, intending to throw her over the cliffs. Had he just taken her along the grey wind-blasted main street that stretches along the A259 like a cadaver on a table, and told her that this is where she was going to have to live with him, she would have jumped of her own accord.

JANE SCOTT

40 MANCHESTER
Vigilans at utilis (Watchful and handy)

Population: 393,000
Unemployment: 5%
Violent crimes: 25.5 (per 1,000 per annum)
% achieving 5 or more GCSE grades A-C: 40.2
Famous residents: Bez, Baby Spice, Morrissey, Nobby Stiles, Terry Christian, Anthony H. Wilson

Manchester is a vibrant, internationally renowned cultural centre and the site of some of the most impressive urban regeneration schemes in British history. That didn't stop hundreds of the famously miserable locals writing to us to complain about it, though.

Don't bother visiting Manchester. Save yourself the time and money and create the Manchester experience in the comfort of your own home. First empty the contents of a litter bin into your shower. Pour yourself a pint of Boddingtons (beer). Stand in shower fully clothed. Switch on shower.

STEPHEN LEWIS

PHOTOS: SAM JORDISON

The brave new Manchester is full of tiny, expensive apartments and terrible bars selling flavoured-for-kids alcopops to coachloads of weekenders arriving from all over the UK. Where it was once the centre of dance culture, the city is now stuffed full of chain bars that look exactly the same and play watered-down-arse-end of house music at an incredible volume.

Not everyone wants to live in a wine-bar strewn, designer-led Posh and Becks world.

Bring back the satanic mills!

JOHN ROBB

39 BRADFORD
Progress, industry, humanity

Population: **468,000**
Unemployment: **4.4%**
Violent crimes: **10 (per 1,000 per annum)**
% achieving 5 or more GCSE grades A-C: **46**
Famous residents:
'Terrorvision', David Hockney, Rita, Sue and Bob Too

Traditionally viewed as a poor relation by residents of Leeds, 'Bradders' has finally managed to beat its pretentious neighbours at something. Shame it was at garnering votes for being crap.

Squalid, dark, dirty and poor. Bill Bryson once said something to the effect that Bradford only exists to make every other town look better. It does this with flying colours.
EDWARD CARDALE

IT'S A RIOT

Bradford has carved a niche for itself in British society, providing many important cultural influences. These include our very own serial killer, the classic '80s adultery film *Rita, Sue and Bob Too* and several high-profile riots.

My favourite part of Bradford is Shipley. With its monolithic 1960s clock tower and charity shop epidemic (where all the posh people from Ilkley dump last season's Jaeger), Shipley has several colourful residents. These include the Shipley Cowboy who stands at Fox's Corner gurning and shooting his fingers into the air, and The Monk who rambles throughout Bradford, rain or shine, in his habit and sandals, waving at cars.
JESSICA

38 MANSFIELD

Sicut quercus virescit industria
(Industry flourishes just like the oak tree)

Population: **98,000**
Unemployment: **4.4%**
Violent crimes: **14**
(per 1,000 per annum)
Famous residents:
Alvin Stardust, Lord Byron, Lord Byron's bear

It used to be thought that Byron kept wild animals for fun. Acquaintance with his modern neighbours suggests, however, that it was probably for security.

I heard that until recently Mansfield was the largest town in Britain with no railway station. It still has that feeling of being cut off and insular. When asking for directions I expected people to tell me to 'keep to the path'. The trains to Nottingham are still pretty scarce (perhaps the good burghers of that city have successfully campaigned to keep the 'Fielders' out).

The football ground looks like one of the pictures you see of a ground belonging to a club that went out of the League 20 years ago. Culture begins and ends with bingo, and the local pastime is hanging around the bus station.

I spent three hours in Mansfield. It was too much. I still have nightmares.

ANDY COYNE

RURAL MANSFIELD

To its credit, Mansfield is surrounded by woodland, and if you've had your car stolen it should be your first port of call. It's also the place to go if you collect broken furniture, tools, kitchen appliances, etc., and if you stay for long enough (five minutes usually does the trick), you'll also get to see the local youths enjoying a spot of joyriding through the trees in a stolen Astra. If you're lucky it might even be yours!

TERESA BODEN

TOO MUCH IS NOT ENOUGH

Andy Coyne is wrong: three hours isn't long enough to judge a town. Had he made an effort to spend a little more time here, he would have experienced the true horror.

Recently, Mansfield came top of the league in the East Midlands for crime. That must be violent crime, as anything with any monetary value was either stolen, smashed up or set fire to, long ago.

NS

PHOTO: SAM JORDISON

37 NEWBURY
Forward Together

Population: **28,000**
Unemployment:
1.7%
Violent crimes: **4.5**
(per 1,000 per
annum)
% achieving 5 or
more GCSE grades A-C: **69**
Famous residents: **Keith
Chegwin, Bruno Brooks,
Andrew Lloyd Webber**

*At first sight there isn't much to
complain about in this attractive
market town, close to the rural
beauties of the Vale of the White
Horse. You have to spend time
there to realise how ghastly it is.*

I visited Newbury when I was
doing my first job in London for
an architectural firm. They'd
been commissioned to build
new offices for Vodafone, the
town's biggest employer. My
task was to move furniture
around on a floor plan to try

PHOTOS: SAM JORDISON

and fit more people into a call centre.

I went to visit the office into which I was squeezing those poor souls, only to discover that Vodafone owned the town, soup to nuts. The bus that I caught from the station was even owned by Vodafone and put on, I can only assume, for the purpose of moving the herds of commuter cattle from their trains to desks, to minimise the risk of anyone making a break for it. I began to suspect that some Vodafone sniper would have picked off any escapees from the top of a Vodafone-owned medieval church tower anyway.

The sad thing was that the centre looked like quite a nice market town – only every signboard hanging from the shops seemed to bear a familiar red and white logo.

It was a while ago now, but I am occasionally kept awake at night by the thought that there might even have been a Vodafone pub.

Years later, in an attempt to

exorcise such horrific thoughts from my mind, I googled Newbury. One of the first things I uncovered was a report detailing objections against those very headquarter buildings that I had helped design. Reading between the lines, it seemed that if Vodafone hadn't been granted planning permission to build these (extremely nice) buildings on a greenfield site, they would leave the town altogether.

It was quite a shock when I subsequently read in the architectural press that the new headquarters building had been completed and Vodafone could now withdraw its staff from 51 locations in Newbury town centre.

I have no idea what has seeped in to replace this commercial vacuum as I have never plucked up enough courage to return. I know that if Newbury is crap then it's partly my fault.

DAN GIBBONS

36 LEICESTER
Semper eadem (Always the same)

Population: **280,000**
Famous residents:
Mark Morrison (The Mac), Gary Lineker, Maggie Philbin, Joe Orton, Some People Who Were On Big Brother

If a town if best described by its people, then Leicester is a large drunk man throwing chicken burger wrappers into the street.

BEN ATHERTON

35 MILTON KEYNES
By knowledge, design and understanding

Population: **207,000**
Unemployment: **3%**
Violent crimes: **10 (per 1,000 per annum)**
% achieving 5 or more GCSE grades A-C: **57**
Famous residents: **Concrete cows**

Etched onto paper in 1962, Milton Keynes was conceived as a means of dealing with the acres and acres of wasteful, ugly countryside in the middle of Buckinghamshire. Soon it became a popular destination for London overspill and one of the country's most infamous new towns.

With the empirical evil of ancient Rome as one of Milton Keynes's major influences, developers cottoned on to the idea of a grid network of completely straight roads, a criss-cross utopia of horizontally and vertically interlocking avenues and boulevards with exciting, futuristic names like H9 Groveway.

Traffic congestion became a major problem, but this was quickly solved by the implantation of roundabouts left, right and centre. The roundabouts helped to disperse

ALL MILTON KEYNES PHOTOS: SAM JORDISON

the soul-crippled, traffic-halting majority, and have ensured that the motorists of Milton Keynes have access to a wide variety of different shapes to look at on their way to work.

An attempt to rebuild the pyramids was MK's next project, as the ribbon of The Point complex was cut. Dressed as a neon-red, spindly metal Walnut Whip, and visible at night from up to ten miles away, this was daft, ugly architecture on a scale never before seen.

Lately, a new £3 million theatre complex has allowed Milton Keynes to attract stars of the calibre of Gary Wilmot and Toyah Wilcox, who distract residents with their irreverently scripted panto-patter.

There are still a few villages in the surrounding areas, and a few remnants of ye olde historie on the outskirts, but no matter, for Milton Keynes is an ever-expanding force of immeasurable power. Freshly augmented by a wad of Prescott-cash, MK shall continue to expand. One day it

may even become a real city. Until then, locals shall have to make do with its boring old New Town status, tapering over the aching in their souls by adorning their Volvos with 'I ♥ MK' stickers, driving around and around the roundabouts, wondering whether to spin the wheel and end it all by H9 ... only resisting because they know how much insurance their despised spouses will get.

ALLAN HARRISON

LOST

My family moved to Milton Keynes in the early 1980s, just as it was being completed, and we thought ourselves very superior as we had a house, whereas the rest of the population seemed to be dwelling in half-built, tin-roofed shacks.

As a teenager I idled away the

hours sitting outside McDonalds helping my friends scavenge for cigarette butts, before graduating to downing Thunderbird in the one decent park. The only excitement to be had was helping my friends lift other friends into waiting ambulances.

CRAP TOWN TRIVIA Milton Keynes shopping centre appeared in the roller-disco inspired video for Cliff Richard's *Wired For Sound*. Then 'The Style Council' wrote a song about the town that included the lyrics 'gonna slash my wrists tonight'.
THANKS TO 'MEL' AND STEVE TATE

What was there to add to this paucity of entertainment? Well, sober Saturdays involved some major choices. Bowling then cinema, or cinema then bowling.

On either side of the town centre there are rows of identical housing estates, mirroring each other in every way, right down to the abandoned shopping trolleys. The most exciting thing that ever happened to me in MK, therefore, was to walk home drunk and find myself in front of an identical house, on an identical street, only to find I was on the wrong estate.

If only I'd grown up in Luton ...

NAOMI ROVNICK

34 TOTTON

Population: **169,000**
Unemployment: **2**
Violent crimes: **6 (per 1,000 per annum)**
Famous residents: **Barry Mung**

ALL TOTTON PHOTOS: A TAYLOR

Totton was once proud to be 'Britain's largest village' until this accolade was stolen from it by unwelcome outside forces, and it became just another crap town.

What Totton still does have to this day is the world's ugliest houses. Stone cladding, pebbledash, Georgian and lead bars, even something that looks scarily like wattle and daub. Every crime against a house front can be found side by side on the same street, many of these innovations combined on the same house.

Totton Conservative Club stands grandly in the town centre. William Hague did claim that the average Tory voter lives in a pebbledash house. In Totton they paint them lime green.

A. TAYLOR

33 BEDFORD
Pride in Bedford

Population: **148,000**
Unemployment: **3.1%**
Violent crimes: **10.4 (per 1,000 per annum)**
% achieving 5 or more GCSE grades A-C: **64**
Famous residents: **Eddie 'The Eagle' Edwards, Terry 'The Prisoner' Waite**

A flat town on the flat lands east of Milton Keynes, Bedford is subject to frequent and dramatic flooding. Global warming has put its future in doubt. We can only hope for the best.

Bedford seems to be twinned with half of Northern Europe – Bamberg included. A few years ago, the fine residents of Bamberg came to visit. One of them was murdered in the foyer of a hotel. Makes us look good, doesn't it?

The Queen came to visit, too. The council only seemed to repave the side of the street she was going to walk along, and only paint the council houses she was going to walk past. I hate the Queen. I hate the council. I hate Bedford. QED.

JEREMY ROBINSON

GOTHIC HORROR
The name of the town has been carried far and wide on the front of Bedford vans, which were never built there.

'It's a rugby town,' proclaim some of the residents proudly. Bizarrely, however, it was home to a large Goth population in the 1980s. Some of them can still be seen, virtually transparent now, flitting between the Bear and Esquires on a Saturday night.

For the rest of the civilians, a visit to Milton Keynes or Luton is regarded as a 'treat'.

DOUG F

32 CROYDON ▽15

Ad summa nitamur (Let's try our best)

Population: 331,000
Unemployment: 4%
Violent crimes: 18.7 (per 1,000 per annum)
% achieving 5 or more
GCSE grades A-C: **64**
Famous residents: **Nestlé, Kate Moss, Ronnie Corbett**

I went to Croydon for a job interview at an employment agency a few months ago. After it was over, I chatted to the lady who interviewed me about what it was like to work in Croydon. She replied, 'It's OK. But we have had two sexual assaults and one shooting in our car park so far this year.' It was still January.

RAY

CRAP TOWN UPDATE

Position last time: 15 ▼

Reasons: *Floor littered with KFC chicken bones like some ancient ancient caveman dwelling. The danger of being poked in the eye with half-snouted cigarettes*

Recent developments:

• *The district auditor has announced that Croydon Council has been spending beyond its means 'for some years' and is about to run out of reserves.*

• *A 90 million-year-old fossil was found in a Croydon man's back garden*

• *Croydon's annual carnival was called off due to 'lack of interest' from sponsors.*

44

31 WOKING

Fide et diligentia (By faith and diligence)

Population: **90,000**
Unemployment: **2%**
Violent crimes: **9 (per 1,000 per annum)**
% achieving 5 or more GCSE grades A-C: **69**
Famous residents: **Paul Weller, Shakin' Stevens, H.G. Wells**

Woking owes most of its development, and unique charm, to the fact that it was chosen as the site for a national cemetery in the nineteenth century.

The first thing you will notice when you leave Woking train station is a sign that reads: 'Welcome to Woking, Home to All-Weather Shopping'.

You will then be confronted by an underground thoroughfare, which you must go through to get into the town proper. This being part of the main route for a legion of WKD swilling, YSL-shirted young Herberts, the passage is permeated by the stench of piss, puke and rotting kebabs.

Thus you will be initiated into Woking culture with a game played by all of its inhabitants – trying to hold your breath long enough to make it out onto the steps at the other side.

So perhaps it is that – the noxious cocktail, the *Eau de Gutter* – that causes the synapses in your brain to click and shudder or perhaps quite simply, the other end of the tunnel really does open out upon some whole new dimension. A new dimension where morality and intelligent thought become redundant (or are 'fucked off out the window' in Woking-speak). Whatever it is, when in Woking you are subject to some terrible evil force.

So you are alone, alone to shop, whatever the weather unless there's a very heavy downpour, in which case the

CRAP TOWN TRIVIA One of Woking's most famous residents, H.G. Wells, featured the town in his novel *The War of the Worlds* – as Martians blew the hell out of it. The writer used to cycle around the town taking great pleasure in planning what would be destroyed next.

public conveniences tend to flood. You wander around the Peacock Centre aimlessly, and find yourself being hypnotised by pan-piped 'Roxette'.

The rain beats down rhythmically on the roof, and the toilets slowly overflow and 'Roxette' is 'Dressed for Success', in some kind of Bolivian poncho by the sounds of it, and you know, deep down, that you may never leave.

SARAH JANES

IN DEFENCE OF WOKING

HUMFREY MALINS C.B.E., M.P.

HOUSE OF COMMONS
LONDON SW1A 0AA

25th March 2004

Dear Sam

Catch any town in wet weather and you won't like it, but there is another side to Woking, which I am proud to represent in Parliament.

The shopping is terrific – there is an excellent hotel in the town centre. Woking boasts an ambitious football team (well worth watching) who play very close to an outstanding leisure centre. There are plenty of places of historical interest to have a look at – for example, the oldest mosque in Britain and the most interesting and famous cemetery at Brookwood. Woking has strong links with H G Wells, author of War of the Worlds, and it was in Woking and its surrounding villages that the Martians in that story land. The town is served by terrific transport links and at no stage are you far from very attractive countryside.

There are many attractions in the town and the surrounding area and I enclose some copy pages from the Borough Council website which I hope you'll find useful.

I can't remember a town I enjoyed visiting when it was raining, but my goodness catch Woking on a nice day, and there's plenty to do, plenty to see and a lot of fun to be had.

Yours sincerely

Humfrey Malins CBE MP

*& r a wonderful
Theatre*

30 PRESTON
Unitate praestans
(Excelling in unity)

Population: 130,000
Unemployment: 3.4%
Violent crimes: 9.9
(per 1,000 per annum)
Famous residents:
Kenny Baker (aka R2D2), Robert Peel (police pioneer), John Inman

My fellow Prestonions won't thank me for sticking the boot into Preston, but I thought what the hell? Prestonions have put the boot into me often enough.

A few years back there was a particularly nasty incident on Preston's main drag, Fishergate, involving a man's head and a plate glass window. The *Lancashire Evening Post* asked on behalf of the police if anybody had witnessed the attack. The newspaper carried a description of the assailant. He was described as being 'in his thirties or forties. Dark haired. Stockily built. Around 6 foot tall and naked'.

CHRIS C

CRAP TOWN TRIVIA *In 1965 KFC chose Preston to be the site of their first UK restaurant.* **RACHEL HALL**

29 ALDERSHOT
Pugna pro patria (Fight for your country)

Population: **30,000**
Unemployment: **2%**
Violent crimes: **11 (per 1,000 per annum)**
Famous residents: **Charles Kingsley (author of *The Water Babies* and commentator on urban development)**

The self-proclaimed 'Home of the British Army'. As a child, the macho world of the army seemed quite appealing. But as I got older and started to venture out in the town after dark, the average British squaddie became a bogeyman.

The paratroop regiments finest are dehumanised, trained to kill, poorly paid and reduced to taking out their pent up aggression on the locals. Pubs and clubs in nearby Camberley ban them, as they even outdo the locals for mindless violence. But the bars in Aldershot are their territory. God forbid the hapless local who walks too close to an open pool-room window, lest they get a glass lobbed at them with the accuracy you'd expect from people trained to throw grenades for a living.

CHRIS WAREHAM

28 BOGNOR REGIS
To excel

Population: 22,000
Unemployment: 2.2%
Violent crimes: 10.2 (per 1,000 per annum)
Famous residents: **Leslie Crowther, William Smith** (holder of the record for building the world's smallest submarine)

Legend has it that George IV's last words were 'Bugger Bognor' when he was told that he would soon have a chance to visit the town. We later generations should have heeded his advice and left the place to the seagulls. Now, the only thing of note in Bognor is the annual 'birdman' event where the locals throw themselves off the pier in a futile attempt to escape.

Even the name is vaguely onomatopoeic and sounds somehow indecent. What is it

about these Victorian coastal towns that is so utterly vulgar and depressing? Is it the fact that they all look exactly the same, with their long-faded grandeur, endless fish and chip shops and gaudy amusement arcades desperate to tempt suckers inside with 'Niagara Falls' of 2p pieces, dementia-inducing electronic cacophony and epileptic neon?

I suppose Bognor is just representative of all these generic seaside towns that drape themselves along our coastline, like over-made-up knackered old tarts soliciting for trade.

It also has the distinction of being one of the foremost towns on Britain's 'Skeleton Coast'. People from all over the British Isles retreat south in their twilight years towards the sea, in some bizarre reversal of evolution, to die. After Ford XRI's, the most common car seen about town is the hearse. Droops of grannies can be seen stopping to watch them pass, and with knowing nods they point and speculate who might be inside. The dual role of this town as both a holiday resort and God's waiting room always struck me as somehow inappropriate.

Kids in cheap sportswear perch like feral pigeons on the railings lining the prom, with their backs to the sea, spitting oysters of phlegm in front of the feet of passing pedestrians. Beneath greasy peaks of baseball caps, they suck on badly rolled joints and try to contort their acne-ravaged features into their interpretation of the hard bastard's thousand-yard stare. Their idea of high comedy is to take the piss out of passing groups of mentally ill children down from Croydon on a day trip.

ANON

LOCAL LOVELIES

If you take a pleasant evening stroll along the promenade in Bognor, you're likely to be asked for drugs, mugged or attacked by seagulls. Step into a local pub or club and prepare to be intimidated by a bevy of local lovelies, dressed largely in skin-tight leopard print and knee high boots – take heed, they may look harmless but they will happily gouge your eyes out with a false red nail if you so much as glance in their direction or in the direction of their fiancé Darren.

SLINKY FAIRY

27 **AIRDRIE**
Vigilantibus (Ever wary)

Population: 36,000
Unemployment: 5%
Violent crimes: 4.3
(per 1,000 per annum)

% achieving 5 or
more GCSE grades

A–C: 28

Stuck on a featureless patch of rain-sodden peat between the most desolate part of Glasgow's East End and the battleship-grey facades of Cumbernauld, Airdrie is famous for two things: alcohol consumption and football hooligans.

> **CRAP TOWN TRIVIA** *Teachers in schools in the Airdrie and North Lanarkshire area were subjected to an average of more than two violent attacks per day between 2002 and 2003.*

Airdrie's sport is football hooliganism, with the notorious Section B. You may remember that minor league Scottish game when the supporters of a club about to go out of business came onto the pitch, broke the crossbar and had the game abandoned. That was Section B.

The drink of Airdrie is Buckfast, a 12% proof tonic wine created in Devon by the Monks of Buckfast Abbey. When Local MP Helen Liddell campaigned against it, its sales are said to have rocketed by 200%. Airdrie now, along with neighbours Coatbridge, accounts for 80% of worldwide Buckfast sales. Can't help wondering what the monks think about it.

For nightlife you can't beat Airdrie's premier Nite Klub (sic) the Double A. With only fluorescent lights (no other ones) and flashing dance floor, à la *Saturday Night Fever*, the phrase 'Day-Glo Hell' is often thrown in its direction. I once left Double A with my face smeared with blood. It wasn't my blood and I still haven't worked out how it got there.

Culture in Airdrie is colourful to say the least – if by colourful you mean Orange. With the

biggest ever Orange Order march held here a few years ago, many a summer evening is filled with the sound of flutes screeching some sectarian ditty. I tend to stay in those weekends. (The Catholics also have their Hibs walks; just change the sentiment above to Green and you get the idea. I stay in on those weekends as well.)

MANI LEOPARD

26 BRISTOL
Virtute et industria
(Manliness and hard work)

Population: **381,000**
Unemployment: **3.1%**
Violent crimes: **16**
(per 1,000 per annum)
% achieving 5 or more GCSE grades
A-C: **58**
Famous residents: **Tricky, Baldrick, Cary Grant**

A town built on the profits of slavery and cigarettes and the ancestral home to some of Britain's wickedest families, Bristol has a rich heritage in moral bankruptcy.

Spurred on by the success of its immediate neighbour, Bath, Bristol attempted to gain recognition as a World Heritage City. That is, until there was no escaping the fact – Bristol's success was achieved by the wholesale theft of live humans from distant countries, and

then the transportation and, finally, the sale of said people resulting in slavery, abject misery, abuse and death.

What's changed?

Well, loads if you could be vaguely bothered to look within the outer ring of characterless, drab, thoughtlessly designed industrial and more recently emerging residential estates. 'Designed with innovation toward the spirited new millennium,' the architects declared. Translated into reality this means, 'It looks shite'.

With an economy that relied on slavery, cancer-causing products and smuggling, it's hardly surprising that Bristol now feels it has something to prove. Sadly it has failed and instead achieved a sprawling conurbation of squalid back streets, incestuous businesses and a notorious envy of its immediate neighbour. With little or no tourist industry, its tourist information cites that one of the most worthwhile attractions is Bath. Unless, of course, you wish to visit other famous Bristol landmarks such as Ikea, the bottom of the M32, or the great Isambard Kingdom Brunel iron ship The Great Briton – now serving burger, chips and coke.

Last but not least, let's not forget the late, great Bristol actor, Cary Grant, who loved Bristol so much that as soon as he had the funds he legged it to America never to return.

IAN HAYWARD

LIMP FOUNTAINS

Bristol – or Brizzle – as the locals call it, was bombed senseless in the Second World War and whatever charm it had prior to that (the ships, the slave trade) has been buried beneath a wave of bizarre planning decisions. Take the centre of the city. It used to be the harbour, but they covered it up with some hapless Ground Force style decking and peculiarly limp fountains, described by a local councillor as looking like '20 old men pissing in a pond'.

JOSIE HUGHES

25 BANGOR

Population: 12,000

'Didn't we have a lovely time the day we went to Bangor?'
No.

KIT CHAMPNESS

24 PORTSMOUTH
Heaven's light our guide

Population: **187,000**
Unemployment: **3%**
Violent crimes: **17.7 (per 1,000 per annum)**
% achieving 5 or more GCSE grades A–C: **36.5**
Famous residents: **Charles Dickens, Freddie Mercury, Peter Sellers, Arthur Conan Doyle, H. G. Wells**

THE LONG OVERDUE DEMOLITION OF THE TRICORN CENTRE

The striking thing about Portsmouth is that it has a natural harbour that is probably the equal of Sydney, but instead of building an opera house and a bridge, they have blotted out the view with crumbling 1960s and early 1970s concrete memorials to the folly of

CRAP TOWN UPDATE

Position last time: **11** ▼
Reasons: *Brown sea. Stony beach. Depressed tourists. Kebab wars. Gnawing, dripping feeling of dread.*
Recent developments:

● *Local MP Mike Hancock's extravagant claim that 'Portsmouth is the cultural capital of the world' was given more substance by the discovery that Turner's famous painting, once listed as Festive Lagoon Scene Venice, actually depicted some pompous old fools arriving at Portsmouth harbour.*

● *Meanwhile, the council have vastly improved the town centre by knocking large parts of it down. Demolition work on the Tricorn Centre was halted almost as soon as it began, however, when contractors discovered it was full of rats and pigeons which had to be exterminated to prevent a plague of fleas from being released into the town.*

town planners from this era. Then they have lined the beautiful Downs overlooking it with mile after mile of three-bedroom semis and council houses. Thus, instead of enhancing something that could be stunning, they have created an edifice to the gobsmackingly cruddy.

IAN CROSSAN

A LOAD OF OLD SHIP

The city is home to a historic dockyard. Historic, I suppose, because it has totally failed to enter the twentieth century and now lies rotting, raising itself occasionally to slap a coat of paint on a Korean freighter.

Apart from HMS *Victory*, the only other museum the local residents bang on about is the *Mary Rose*. Truth be told, this is little more than a railway sleeper lying in a big tent with a hose permanently played on it.

'LORD NELSON'

HARD-HITTING

Within six months of moving to Portsmouth, I was beaten up by some colourful locals for 'opening my coat' to them (whatever that means). My girlfriend was thrown into the road in broad daylight by a complete stranger and then hit by a car, and two Spanish students went to South Parade (virtually on my doorstep at the time) to have a look at the sea and were beaten about the head with planks.

It's not just crap, it's certifiable.

CHRISTOPHER WEBB

IN DEFENCE OF PORTSMOUTH

I think you'd have to be certifiable not to see what a great city Portsmouth is.

COUNCILLOR MIKE HANCOCK
EXECUTIVE MEMBER FOR PLANNING,
REGENERATION, ECONOMIC DEVELOPMENT
AND TOURISM
PORTSMOUTH CITY COUNCIL

[BAD COUNCIL]

The Tricorn Centre is on the way out and Portsmouth has a new landmark, the Spinnaker Tower. It may be beautiful, but it has caused no end of bother. It was supposed to be finished in time for the city's millennium celebrations. It wasn't. The council said it wouldn't cost taxpayers a penny. Now they've had to stump up £8.4 million to bail out the troubled project. Still, it's an impressive building and the view from the top will be awesome - just as soon as they get rid of all the other eyesores around it.

23 WREXHAM

Labor omnia vincit
(Hard work conquers all)

Population: **128,500**
Unemployment: **3.3%**
Violent crimes: **9.4**
(per 1,000 per annum)

"We hate Wrexham," chant the supporters of every other football team in Division Two. The locals, in turn, hate everyone else and this Welsh border town has seen some of the most vicious race riots in British history.

Wrexham is the proud owner of a football club, and nothing else whatsoever since the brewery closed. The brewery used to produce Wrexham Lager, 'The ONLY Welsh lager'. Unsurprisingly, the drink was not popular in the country of Cerys Matthews's birth because it was only about 3% ABV.

ELISA PARISH

[BAD COUNCIL]

When an internal auditor, Andrew Sutton, tried to expose corruption in Wrexham's neighbouring council, Flintshire, he was hounded from his job.

'Shut up or we'll take your fucking head off,' said the group of thugs that approached him on the street in Wrexham.

'You tell Andy to be quiet,' said the six men towering over his friend Ted Francis, an old age pensioner, as he tried to eat his breakfast in a local café.

But Sutton kept at it, revealing that the council had 'hoodwinked' the Welsh Office out of £300,000 for a doomed industrial development – and wasted hundreds of thousands of pounds of their own money into the bargain. He also exposed an illegal payment of £20,000 to the manager of a care home, where it was known that elderly women suffering from dementia had been sexually assaulted.

Then, when he realised that this corruption reached the highest levels of the council, he was sacked. An industrial tribunal recently found in his favour, declaring it 'constructive dismissal' and 'intimidation of a whistleblower'.

HOPE STREET
STRYT YR HÔB

22 PORTADOWN

Population: 21,000
Unemployment: 3.1%

Famous residents: Roy Walker from *Catchphrase*, David Trimble

Portadown is infamous the world over for its sectarian problems and hate-filled marching season.

Once every year, the Orange Order gathers at Drumcree Church and brings along a host of political cavemen to join in the fun.

This is, of course, all in the name of 'protest' about the government's decision to disallow the Order and its vast entourage to march down the Queen's highway, as was. Such a decision has, for years, irked these good citizens who would regularly look forward to scaring small children and families on the contentious estate. All of this is played out in the full glare of the media spotlight, ensuring Northern Ireland and Portadown in particular are not exactly top of the tourist wish-list.

The town itself doesn't let the side down for the remainder of the time. The various flags on lamp-posts add a nice touch of colour to the otherwise dreary surroundings and, on the rare days of sunshine, all manner of people emerge. It is a bit like Burnley but with more tattoos.

M. COYLE

GWYN

21 **WINCHESTER**

Population: **107,000**
Unemployment: **1.6%**
Violent crimes: **6.8 (per 1,000 per annum)**
Famous residents: **David Gower, Jane Austen**

Winchester's ongoing campaign against wildlife and natural beauty reached a new high in 2004, ensuring its continuing ascendancy in the league of shame.

How I agree with your survey on Winchester. But you didn't mention the drunken student population that has nearly overrun the city. We have lived on a nice council estate here for over 30 years and, in the last few, nearly every house coming on to the market has been bought by people who let them out to students. This makes it impossible for the young people that live in the area to find anything that they can afford. As a result, there is no sense of community. The Winchester of old is long gone.
DOROTHY THOMPSON

RIGHT ON

Now I really must protest! Winch is a lovely place. It is one of the four cities I have been to that has 'the oldest pub in England'. The fake Tudor-beams are really something.

I acknowledge that all the shop attendants are rude and that there is not one nightclub. But nowhere is perfect.

Winchester is a good place to live. It produces good Conservatives from a wonderfully selective gene pool.
CHRIS

CRAP TOWN UPDATE

Position last time: 5 ▼

Reasons: *Broken-beer bottle violence. Priggish complacency of inhabitants. Margaret Thatcher and the M3. Posh school kids.*

Recent developments:

• *Tourism chiefs harp on about the 'safety' of the ancient Saxon town, but the police have had to lay on patrols on Friday and Saturday* *nights to stop the privileged locals from tearing each other apart, as well as introducing new on-the-spot fines for yobbish behaviour.*

• *A decade after the M3 was gouged through Twyford Down, the meadowland that was granted to the people of Winchester 'in perpetuity' has been covered over by a car park at the behest of the local council.*

20 PORT TALBOT

Population: 134,000
Unemployment: 4%
Violent crimes: 9 (per 1,000 per annum)
Famous residents: Sir Anthony Hopkins, Richard Burton, Sir Geoffrey Howe (former Tory deputy PM)

Pollution in Port Talbot turns white PVC pink. Small compensation for living in the worst town in Wales.

A big steel works-cum-refinery in the middle of an eerie sulphur-infused lake, surrounded by a few crumbling housing estates. The main landmark is the M4 passing over it and the orange windsock on the side of this which, no matter what the weather, always stands at an angle of 90 degrees, a filth encrusted, stiffened warning flag.

The smell is enough to keep your windows locked tight in August.

MS JUSTINE MARIE DAVIDGE

IN DEFENCE OF PORT TALBOT

It is seriously inaccurate to quote 'ancient' observations about Port Talbot relating to refineries (all now disappeared), the coal industry (the last mine closed in the constituency in 1970) and pollution, traffic and other environmental problems which are more to do with the past than the present. While it would be misleading to state that we are free of these challenges, great improvements have been made in recent times.

Today, in the Western Mail, one of my constituents, Mr Nigel Hunt of Heol Addison, has written very eloquently of the beauty, history and talent of the constituency, referring to Andrew Vicari, Rob Brydon, Michael Sheen and Dick Penderyn. He could have also added Mabon, David Carpanini and Mavis Nicholson, to say nothing of the first Labour Prime Minister, Ramsey MacDonald, who happened to be Aberavon's first Labour MP.

Port Talbot is a fine town, with a great past and a great future. Don't knock it!

HYWEL FRANCIS,
MP FOR ABERAVON AND PROUD OF IT

19 HULL

Population: 224,000
Unemployment: 6%
Violent crimes: 15.3 (per 1,000 per annum)
Famous residents: Philip Larkin, John Prescott

Last time it was Britain's Number 1 crap town. Now it is fallen in the ranks, largely due to a concerted and impressive emailing campaign from local residents who actually enjoy living there. They've convinced us that The Deep, the historical old town and the many oak-beamed pubs are well worth visiting. Unfortunately for Hull though, plenty of people still don't agree.

CRAP TOWN UPDATE

Position last time: 1 ▼
Reasons: *Smells of death. Council spent a fortune doing up homes which were then demolished. Human turd found in a phone box. Silent threat of violence hanging in the air.*

Recent developments:
- *Kingston upon Hull town council was named by the audit commission as the worst in the country.*
- *A recent survey revealed Hull has the highest levels of obesity in the country.*

CHOOSE LIFE

What's more irritating that living in a crap town? Having some jumped-up Southerner tell you it's crap.

CHRIS PEEBLES-BROWN

WHO DO YOU THINK YOU'RE KIDDING?

I won't go into the one about Hull, as it clearly has happy memories for other readers who have chosen to defend it. Fair enough, there were lots of nice, reasonable people who thought Mr Hitler would be a good thing for Germany too.

JOHN BROWN

ACID CASUALTY

Apparently John Betjeman once called it 'a wonderful city of domes and spires', or something like that. He must have been on some seriously heavy hallucinogens at the time.

In reality Hull is a sad story of unemployment, teenage pregnancy, heroin addiction, crime, violence, and rampant self-neglect. I was born and brought up there, but couldn't wait to leave. Why? Because my memories of home are of the flat and boring landscape, the seemingly endless housing estates, the architecture – which is most flatteringly described as 'municipal' in style – and the narrow-minded, bigoted attitudes of the vast majority of the populace.

IAIN ROBERTSON

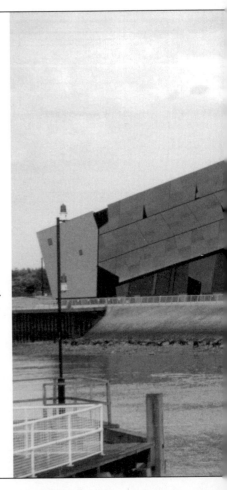

THE DEEP. 'LOVELY'

IN DEFENCE OF HULL

What's all this about Hull being dangerously violent? I must be living a very sheltered life because in my four years in Hull, I have never witnessed a single violent incident. I know there are sometimes late night disturbances involving drunks, but what's new? It is no more dangerous or violent than any other UK town.

I find the people in Hull friendly and helpful. I've never had any problems during the day or night.

Loads of money has been spent regenerating the city with The Deep, a lovely deep-sea world attraction that I have visited twice. They have the new Kingston Communications Stadium, Kingswood retail park which has a cinema, hotel, shops, restaurants, supermarket, etc and it's all set in shrubbery and looks great. They have a nice marina with pubs and cafés nearby.

I've been all over the UK and have been too far worse places than Hull.

ALLIE

18 LITTLEHAMPTON
It's our kind of place

Population: **30,000**
Unemployment: **2.2%**
Violent crimes: **10.2 (per 1,000 per annum)**
% achieving 5 or more GCSE grades A-C: **46**
Famous residents: **Anita Roddick (Body Shop founder), Ronnie Barker, Des Lynam lives not too far away, as does Leo Sayer**

Sex! Seedy south coast sex! The innocent appearance and prurient manners of this cosy boating haven hide a fascinating world of leopard skin clothes and dodgy dancing. It's better than Brighton...

Whenever I was taken to Littlehampton I would wonder why we were there. It would invariably be unsunny and the place was definitely not fun. The only conclusion that I can come up with now was that my mum and dad were swingers, and they had some swinger pals living in the area. I do seem to recall going to a mock Tudor house with a bar in it. If my memory serves me right,

CRAP TOWN TRIVIA

Attempts to open a shop called Adult Attractions in Littlehampton met with furious opposition from local residents. Outraged mother of six, Lynne Scarfe spoke for many when she said: 'I think it's appalling. This is supposed to be a family seaside resort. There were adult videos, blindfolds and other risqué items in the window, and what looked like a rubber basque.'

there was a pineapple-shaped ice bucket and there were brass horse heads all over the place.

Loads of swingers live in Littlehampton. I know this because there's lots of pampas grass in people's front gardens: a sign understood by swingers to mean that there are swingers there. One day, in 1985, my mum and dad dug up their pampas grass and burnt it in a heap in the back garden. After that we never went to Littlehampton again.

However, recently I found myself in Littlehampton again and discovered that it is home to one of the finest pubs ever. It is a perfect glass time-capsule of booze and fag-fuelled 1980s family fun.

PHOTOS: SAM JORDISON

If the generous distribution of leopard skin and unbuttoned shirts is anything to go by, it remains a popular hang-out, I think, of the swingers. There was a disco on. I felt immediately at home as soon as I had crossed the threshold, and had an urgent desire for a Snowball.

My boyfriend and I sat down next to the dance floor, upon which an old fella in a waistcoat was playing some songs on a keyboard. A very bold couple came and did some sexy dancing, white trousers, red dress, very suggestive. The old fella clocked us and asked if we liked 'Oasis'.

Later on in the evening there was a raffle. We won four bottles of Babycham. I knew we would.

Littlehampton, crap but charming.

SARAH JANES

17 LONDON = NON-MOVER

Population: **7 million**
Unemployment: **7%**
Violent crimes: **90.2 (per 1,000 per annum)**
Famous residents: Oliver Twist, Oswald Mosley, Jack the Ripper, Jack Straw

The capital of the UK feeds off the rest of the country like a leech, growing heavier and more ugly by the day.

New government plans will extend its sprawling mass all the way along the Thames, to the North Sea, at the same time as great swathes of our Northern cities are being demolished.

All houses within a five-mile radius of St Paul's are beginning to cost so much money that soon only management consultants and rats will be able to survive there.

CRAP TOWN UPDATE

Position last time: 17 ▣
Reasons: *Too big. Does not swing.*
Dr Johnson was an old windbag.
Unreliable tube.
Recent developments:

• The congestion charge has been a great success, but the part privatisation of the tube has made it even worse than before, and everyone's moaning about the new 'bendy buses' because they take up too much road space and keep catching fire.

• Average house prices rocketed past the £250,000 mark as experts predicted an imminent crash.

• Big Ben broke.

London smells of exhaust fumes, sweat and cheap perfume.

All the famous London landmarks are actually very ugly indeed: St Paul's looks like a dark grey egg in a dirty egg-cup; Parliament looks like an anorexic church; the Telecom Tower (formerly Post Office tower) looks like an extraterrestrial rectal probe.

The tube inflicts misery. It also has its own subculture of 'tube-books' – novels

ALL LONDON PHOTOS: SAM JORDISON

76

that are advertised exclusively on the tube, and are only read by tube-travellers, and will not sell (or be put on sale) anywhere else in the country. Most of these, oddly enough, are 'amusing' fantasy 'novels' about escaping life as a commuter, or about being wealthy (same thing).

GARRICK

YOU'RE WATCHING BIG BROTHER

You have to stay in most nights watching *Big Brother* because London is the only place where you can spend loads of money doing absolutely nothing. If you do go out, it's to some two-bit gastropub where the punters are duped into thinking bangers and mash are the height of cosmo-cool, or to meet tiresome dullards at parties who are attempting to derive kudos from (a) living in London or (b) having a close friend whose ex is a cousin of someone who eats at the Ivy.

The only reason so many people live here is because the UK is on a slope like a bad pool table, and the economic laws of gravity inevitably lead people to roll down here. The answer to the North–South divide? A folded beer mat under Kent.

PETE SEAMAN

16 BRIXTON

Population: **65,000**
Famous residents:
John Major, Skin from 'Skunk Anansie', David Bowie

In the entire time I've lived in Brixton I have only met my next-door neighbours twice. The first time was when I was having a barbeque and they leaned over the fence and said: 'Give us some meat, there's fifteen hungry junkies round here that haven't eaten solids for a week.' The second time was when the police came round to arrest them all and they escaped over the back fence, stashing their drugs in my shed and waving pistols in the air like extras in a Tarantino film. That time I stayed in my kitchen. Since then the house has been boarded up.

I tell my friends that I hate it, but they think I'm just being soft.

'Oh, but the market is just so vibrant,' they say and, 'Everything happens here.' I can only assume they've found some use for used batteries and greying bush meat that I haven't yet come across, and that by 'everything' they mean the ability to buy impure drugs at twice the going rate.

'And you can buy a travel card here for £1.50,' they add, thrilled to the bottom of their ironic Dunlop sneakers to be involved in a criminal racket. But cheap tickets don't compensate for the chaos around the underground station, and for having to run a daily gauntlet of leering crackheads, angry bad boys and olive and ciabbatta crazy Sainsbury's shoppers. All that just to get into its stinking dark tunnels.

Every day, I pray for a raise, just so I can move to Clapham.

OLIVER NEAL

15 CAMDEN

Population:
200,000
Famous
residents:
**Withnail, I,
Shane McGowan**

*The dirt, noise, tie-dyed clothes
and ready availability of bad
drugs make Camden seem
impossibly exciting to a certain
kind of pubescent. Until they
grow up and realise that it just
plain stinks.*

Incense, leather, buckles and
statues of the Buddha. Bongs,
alien heads and records you can
get far cheaper everywhere
else. Podgy teenage girls
tottering around on platform
heals, checking their make-up
(black lipstick, white
foundation) in the lids of their
wacky-baccy tins, wondering if
this is what cool is, and when
they'll find someone who, like,
really understands them.

'Well, I kind of think of myself as more of a
cyber-skate-Goth-hybrid,' they yarl, dragging
deeply on hand-rolled cigarettes, while
lecherous market stallholders eye their breasts
and sell them Tibetan trinkets they've made
themselves from coat hangers and crepe paper.

Down by the canal, a man beckons you over.
'Psssst, hey brother, you like to buy some real

nice mary-huana?' You say no and then notice that his friends are standing around you, grasping their beer cans just a bit too tight. 'It's real good,' he says. 'Moroccan hash.' You give him £20 and he gives you a piece of dark wood wrapped in cling film.

Near the tube, an old man drops his pants and lays a giant cable and nobody bats an eyelid. The shops make huge profits from anti-capitalist culture, the kids feel sick the next day and always, lurking just around the corner, is Kentish Town with its cider and smack and huge Victorian tenement blocks where old tramps go to die.

'MR JONES'

14 HANWELL

Population: **26,000**
Unemployment: **4%**
Violent crimes: **21 (per 1,000 per annum)**
% achieving 5 or more GCSE grades A-C: **48**
Famous residents: **Rick Wakeman (rocker), Charlie Chaplin (went to the local poor school)**

Squashed between the ethnic glitz of Southall and the imperial might of Ealing, 'Queen of Suburbs', Hanwell is a slither of West London that few have heard of and no-one cares about – which is probably why al-Qaida recently chose it as the site for a bomb-making factory.

ALL HANWELL PHOTOS: ANDREW CARNE ROSS

Hanwell's only purpose has been to inspire ways to get through it. Isambard Brunel was compelled to erect a long railway viaduct over the town, while the builders of the Grand Union Canal constructed a set of six consecutive locks, known as the Hanwell Flight, to ease quick passage up to Birmingham.

The only people who stay in Hanwell have little choice in the matter. So many insane people have been sent to Hanwell Lunatic Asylum that the town is now in some dictionaries as another word for madhouse.

Thousands of council tenants were shifted to Hanwell after the war due to the comprehensive redevelopment of

Hanwell was originally named Hanewelle, meaning 'cock frequented stream', deriving from the words (hana) cock and (weille) stream. Most of the area's road drains now go straight into the local river. Oil, paint and dirty water are among the known pollutants that have been tipped into drains by residents and businesses. The water is filthy and polluted. Now the cocks would all be dead.

Paddington. And thousands of tons of rubbish have been dumped next to the Brent River, now re-landscaped as a nature reserve.

Hanwell's standard bearers will herald its clock tower, a grey box that for many years always showed twenty-five to three. But what they should really point to is the fact that Hanwell is where 'Deep Purple' first perfected their hard rock genius.

ANDREW HARRIS

13 KEW

Population:
15,000
Famous
residents:
Orchids and lots and lots of lovely trees

Populated by big bankers with receding hairlines and exploding girths, it's the sticky cherry on top of affluent Richmond's already calorie-filled cake.

Be warned: this sugar is only for the few. Should you enter one of the numerous flowery cafés that flank the tube station, you'll find yourself taking out a mortgage for a croissant and sniffed at by snub-nosed, Alice-banded women (said banker's wives) as you shuffle, broken and skint, to take your seat. There, while the chatter about difficult nannies hums on, waitresses will bang noisily around you and whisk your plate away before you've had time to lick off the last precious crumbs.

Come summer there are hoards of tourists. Not just any tourist, but gangs of middle-aged women who harangue each other with loud, nasal accents. They storm down the road like runaway herds of Laura-Ashley-skirted cattle, grinding old ladies and student-types under giant hooves in their desperation to get to the only natural colour in their bourgeois lives – the orchids from the orchid house.

ELLY MILLAR

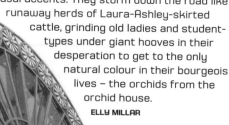

12 HACKNEY

Justitia turris nostra
(Justice is our tower or Our tower is righteous)

Population: **203,000**
Unemployment: **6.6%**
Violent crimes: **31.8 (per 1,000 per annum)**
% achieving 5 or more GCSE grades A-C: **50**
Famous residents: **Eli Hall (deceased)**

The borough was on fire for most of the 2003 summer. Gibbons furniture store, a landmark for a hundred years, has gone, leaving only a smouldering bite mark on Amhurst Road. There was also a blaze at the site of the Eurotunnel ventilation shaft halfway down Graham Road, not far from where Eli Hall immolated himself at the climax of the Hackney siege.

Hackney's psychic weather is a battle between the low-pressure front of gentrification – drifting up from Hoxton and across the preservation area around London Fields and the high pressure above Clapton, which continues to press layers of deprivation and derangement down upon the borough.

If it's not the man at the bus stop inclined over his crack pipe, it's the bag lady walking backwards up Pembury Hill blathering away into a child's oversized red plastic phone. In Lower Clapton, someone taped a crate to a lamppost, bearing the legend 'Psychic baby brain bath'.

The metropolitan bourgeoisie, after a few glasses of red, might roll their eyes at one another and mutter darkly about living close to 'the front line', but the north-eastern corner of the borough, Clapton, is worse than that. It is Interzone; it is down the rabbit-hole wrong. It's the only place I have gone into a newsagent and asked the woman

CRAP TOWN UPDATE

Position last time: 10 ▼

Reasons: *Dangerous and dirty. Men get skinned alive. The council was so corrupt that its own fraud department had to be investigated. There's rubbish everywhere.*

Recent developments:

● *Hackney's failing education services have recently been taken over by a private trust. The transformation has been rapid. In 2003, Hackney recorded the worst overall exam results in the country instead of the second worst.*

● *Local MP Brian Sedgemore was mugged. His assailants made away with a bag of chips.*

● *After opening two years too late, the council's flagship millennium project, the £31 million pound Clissold Leisure Centre, closed after less than two years in operation. Walls had cracked, floors leaked, drains blocked and water poured into electrical fittings. No one knows when it will open again.*

● *Hackney Council has maintained its traditional position in the Top 10 of the Audit Commission's league table of 'worst performers'.*

behind the counter how her weekend went, only for her to reply, 'I died, but they resuscitated me, and now I am back at work.'

The press dubbed the area 'Murder Mile' but that's incidental. You don't need media scare stories, you can just walk around it for ten minutes and be terrified.

The artist and Turner Prize winner Martin Creed emblazoned the phrase 'Everything is going to be alright' across the front of the orphan asylum at the end of Linscott Road, presumably in an attempt to alleviate the dolour. But such laudable artistic intent is undercut by the asylum itself, as all that remains of it is its classical colonnade, a portal into another world. At one time, it offered maintenance and education to nearly 500 children.

These days, Hackney is no longer capable of comforting the afflicted. From all over the world – from Albania to Zaire – people seek asylum here, but all they find is a madhouse.

MATTHEW DE ABAITUA

11 BIRMINGHAM
Forward

Population: 1 million
Unemployment: 6%
Violent crimes: 20 (per 1,000 per annum)
% achieving 5 or more GCSE grades A-C: 58
Famous residents: 'Slade', 'UB40', Ozzy Ozbourne, 'Napalm Death'

Sometimes you find a nice old pub in Birmingham where you can idly sup and unwind, and listlessly ponder. You go back a week later, and it's boarded up and about to be demolished and replaced with a 'mixed-use development'. This means a tall building with rubbish 'café bars' on the ground floor, playing bad music and dispensing insipid Pilsner for three quid a mouthful; and above them overheated open-plan offices where admin. assistants and sales execs compare

ONE COOL NEW SELFRIDGES
BUILDING AND A FEW AL FRESCO
CAFES DO NOT MAKE UP FOR
DECADES OF NEGLECT AND
CRIMES AGAINST THE HUMAN EYE

ringtones and baguettes, and snigger about Anne Summers parties.

The rest of Birmingham is following suit, with shiny shoes and Ben Sherman shirts. Consequently, the not-too-arsed vibe that made the city quite a cool place in the late 1980s and early '90s is no more. Birmingham today differs from all the other menacing, intolerant, highly strung towns nominated, only it's loads bigger.

The 'developers' responsible for these things paint words and pictures on the boards that fence off the building works, to tell you what they're doing. Just now, one of these reads: 'Birmingham – set to become one of the best cities in the world'. Let us leave aside speculation as to the intended audience and purpose of this masterpiece of subjectivity. Let us simply reflect that if it bore the remotest grain of truth, it would not need to be there.

PETE GREEN

CRAP TOWN TRIVIA
The Birmingham accent is the worst accent in the UK for your career according to a recent survey by image consultants The Aziz Corporation. Meanwhile, Country Life readers have voted Birmingham New Street Station the second most hated eyesore in the country.

MIDDLESBROUGH
Erimus (We will be)

Population: **135,000**
Unemployment: **6%**
Violent crime: **7.1 (per 1,000 per annum)**
% achieving 5 or more GCSE grades A-C: **42**
Famous residents: **Roy Chubby Brown, Paul Daniels, Chris Rea, Ridley Scott**

Most of Middlesbrough's once mighty industrial temples are now home only to the wind. A few jobs are provided by a huge chemical works, but this also makes the city stink from dawn until dusk.

It is interesting to hear some of the misapprehensions that people Not From The North East hold of the area.

They may refer to a warm and friendly welcome. They may enthuse about the accent. Career-students might enthusiastically pipe up about the topic of the cost of beer. Someone who has replaced his or her life with football might also interject, to inform you of its Premiership-status team.

Unfortunately, with the immediacy of a javelin poked sadistically through the spokes of someone's speeding motorcycle, this is where these facile and hopelessly optimistic statements must end.

'A warm and friendly welcome'

I'm keen to point out that in fact, at least among strangers, the warm welcome rarely exists. I've been beaten-up for a cigarette.

'Nice accent'

The real Middlesbrough accent, it seems, is the blighted child of a Scouse

father and a mother who has mild traces of Newcastle in her accent. It is more evident in the younger generation what the true sound of the accent is, and it usually sounds like it's going to scrounge ten pence from you or steal your bike.

'Cheap beer'

If you are a student, then the University of Teesside's Student Union might be the place for you. Here, you might find that the assertion of 'cheap beer' holds true. This is just a protective bubble, a false community of students, by students, for students. Step outside this bubble, and beer-prices are roughly in line with most of the North of the UK.

To drink in the town itself, at least as a student, is a risky affair. To drink outside the town is simply suicidal.

'Good football team'

If you support a team that is not Middlesbrough, then you have two choices:

(a) don't go to Middlesbrough

(b) change your allegiance.

MARK WINGATE

IT'S A SCREAM

Last November I visited Middlesbrough for a few days on business. I checked in at the hotel on the Thursday, and was politely and helpfully informed by the young lady at the desk that it wasn't a good idea to go out in the centre of 'Boro after dark. I mistakenly assumed that this was just another method of

persuading guests to use the hotel's facilities in the hope of raking in yet more cash. So, I thought, I would pop out early evening and find a quick bite to eat before an early night. Bad idea.

Let's just say if you aren't from 'Boro don't go into a pub and order a pint (remember that bit in the old Westerns when the gunman walks in and the piano stops playing?).

Despite having to kick a syringe out of the way on the way back to the hotel, I did survive the evening. I only woke up once in the night as well and that was just because of the screaming. I looked out of the window and saw a body on the paving below.

As it happens I was there to talk to members of the local police force, and the description from one officer (though I doubt it's the official line) was memorable: 'Two things to do in Middlesbrough. Chemical industry and crime. The second is easier to get into and you aren't any more likely to be killed by it.'

GUY SANSOM

IN DEFENCE OF MIDDLESBROUGH

All in all, Middlesbrough isn't too bad. There are worse places to live, but I would recommend that you stay out of Middlesbrough at night, and during the day stick to the main streets.

ANON

CORBY
Deeds not words

Population: **51,00**
Unemployment: **3.7%**
Violent crime: **17.1 (per 1,000 per annum)**
% achieving 5 or more GCSE grades A-C: **46**
Famous residents: **Bill Drummond, Lemmy from 'Motorhead', Brandan Reilly (Olympic high jumper), Sir Matt Busby didn't come from Corby, although half the buildings in the town are named after him**

A new town that's ageing very badly, Corby is the bulging grey wart on Northamptonshire's otherwise beautiful countenance. Its bleak central precinct is crumbling, its surrounding industries have departed and its people have few reasons to stay.

Corby is the result of a hideous plot to despoil the otherwise thoroughly pleasant East Midlands. When the huge steel works was built there were nothing like enough people in the surrounding villages and leather industry towns to operate it. In a clever bit of town planning, thousands of Glaswegian steel workers were relocated to rural England, to live in a newly constructed town whose chief attraction, at least to today's visitor, appears to have been its similarity to 1930s Glasgow.

When the factory closed down in the early 1980s, what was left was a staggeringly depressing small industrial town, no jobs, and no likelihood of getting any: cue the most spectacularly unsuccessful series of New Town urban renewal schemes ever witnessed.

On the plus side, if you like abattoir floor sweepings, you've got a much better chance of finding haggis or Scotch pie in a chip shop in Corby than in any town for miles and miles and miles around.

GREG JACK

CRAP TOWN TRIVIA

- Corby is the largest town in Europe without a train station.
- It has one of the highest rates of underage pregnancy in the country.
- It was the first town in England to trial dusk to dawn curfews for teenagers.
- Poet and prize-winning author John Burnside, who lived in Corby as a teenager, is rumoured to have completed his English O-level exam in just 20 minutes and still achieved a grade A. However, he was soon after expelled from school for smoking jazz cigarettes. He later said Corby was 'really strange', describing the steel works as 'a suburb of Hell'. He set a novel in the town, calling it *Living Nowhere*.

In the early 1980s, Corby Council embarked on a huge regeneration project to reclaim polluted land. Twenty years later, the work was still unfinished, and the police had run a series of investigations into allegations of criminal acts in connection with handing out the land contracts, and an Audit Commission report identified 'systematic weaknesses' within the council system for managing contracts. It highlighted 'non-existent and frequently poor' checks and controls over payments, and several areas in which councillors could be 'open to allegations of collusion with contractors'.

Now, when you click onto the regeneration section of Corby Council website, you're taken to a picture of a bunch of Lego skate-boarders hanging out next to a wheelie-bin. What can it all mean?

[BAD COUNCIL]

CUTTING IT

Corby still makes steel, but not as much as it used to. A few years back British Steel repeated the town's early history by convincing a lot of Scots, from Ravenscraig, to come down and make steel as their own works were to be closed. This was another false dawn, and with their resulting redundancy money many set up taxicab firms presumably specialising on finding ways out of Corby. Thus you see no buses. And you are constantly being cut up by other drivers.

HARVEY EDGINGTON

IT'S MURDER

Corby was the first place outside Scotland to see the launch of alcoholic Irn Bru. Lucky us.

I went to school with two 12-year-old murderers, both girls.

CHRIS

IT'S GRIM UP
NORTHAMPTONSHIRE

CLIMBING THE GREASY POLE

Every 20 years they hold a strange festival called the Corby pole-fair.

Apart from the hastily erected bungee crane (which makes locals imagine how good it would be if it didn't involve a rope, or bouncing back), the main attraction is the aforementioned pole. It stands in the middle of a park, tall, proud and greased, and anyone can try and climb it to win the top prize of a ham.

I looked on at the competitors with sympathy. The game was a poignant microcosm for life in Corby because, try as they might, no one could scale the damned thing, just as no one could escape the murky depths of the troubled town.

TOM MORIARTY

8

NOTTINGHAM
Vivit post funera virtus
(Virtue lives on after death)

Population: **267,000**
Unemployment: **5.2%**
Violent crime: **26.2 (per 1,000 per annum)**
% achieving 5+ GCSE grades A-C: **46**
Famous residents: **Robin Hood, Harold Shipman, Sue Pollard, Torville and Dean**

In the past, Robin Hood hated Nottingham so much he took to the trees and dedicated his life to trying to kill the local sheriff. The council have just spent £200 million on a futuristic tram system, but the problems of the present – the gangs and the guns – won't go away.

The awful truth is that the 'Queen of the Midlands' has been on a life-support machine since the 1980s. We have spiralling gun crime, under-performing schools and, for a city that once prided itself on its diverse manufacturing output, absolutely no industry – unless you consider call centres and bar work to be meaningful forms of employment.

The famous Nottingham Castle isn't a castle at all, but a crumbling and neglected Victorian stately home and garden, overrun with rats and disappointed American tourists.

To top it all, we have a city council whose incompetence and stupidity knows no bounds. Several years ago, they thought it would be a good idea to dump 10 tonnes of sand in the Market Square and pass it off as 'Nottingham by the Sea'.

What?

A recent nationwide survey concluded that Nottingham was one of the unhappiest cities in the UK.

Can you blame us?

ROBERT TURNER

CRAP TOWN TRIVIA

St Ann's, in Nottingham, was the first place in the UK where police carried out routine armed patrols. The city's Queen's Medical Centre contains Europe's busiest Accident and Emergency unit, and deals with more gunshot wounds than any other hospital in the UK.

CRAP TOWN TRIVIA

A rumour was once published that you were five times more likely to die of unnatural causes if you stood outside the KFC on Alfreton Road, in Radford, Nottingham, than anywhere else in the country. Admittedly, a preposterous statistic, but I've seen the bloody, tragic reality behind it.

My doctor's surgery is around the corner from that street and once, on my way there, I passed an area cordoned off, swarming with police – in the street, a pool of blood saturated a tangled mess of clothing on the pavement. The next day I read that an hour previous to my passing, a cyclist was shot twice by a rival gang. That pool must have been no more than 20 yards from the KFC.

TOM

DON'T BELIEVE THE HYPE

Nottingham is ridiculously over-hyped. The local council proclaim 'our style is legendary'. A radio station announces every ten minutes that we are in 'The World's Best City'. Even *Lonely Planet* says it's one of the most 'liveable (and visitable) of British cities'.

I, however, tend to agree more with my mate Bob Jones who points out that there have been three murders on his road in the last six months, that anyone taking a radio inside the city limits is statistically more liable to have it stolen than in just about anywhere else in the world, and that most of the buildings around him are uglier than a rectal prolapse.

CHRIS AITKEN

BATH

Floreat Bathon (Let Bath flourish)

Population: **169,00**
Unemployment: **2%**
Violent crime: **7 (per
1,000 per annum)**
% achieving 5 or more
GCSE grades A-C: **66**
Famous residents: **Van
Morrison, Hugh Grant, the
guitarist from 'Tears For
Fears', Jamie Cullum**

*Bath, with its famous honey
yellow stone, Georgian
architecture and magnificent
Roman remains, is an undeniably
beautiful city, spoilt only by the
imposition of some brutally ugly
1960s architecture, brutally
expensive house prices and a few
generally brutal inhabitants.*

Essentially a retirement town with an unpleasant amount of students, Bath also contains an abundance of people approaching 30 still living at home and getting stoned every night.

Music is banned, and there seems to be a law stating that all clubs must be situated below ground, have dripping ceilings and serve expensive, flat beer.

Even its revered Georgian architecture has been attacked by the short-sighted, mean-spirited local council. The centre of this beautiful city is basically a concrete trench lined with McDonalds and vicious teenagers idly playing with lock knives.

In the summer, it fills to the brim with loud tourists who clog the narrow streets like the coagulated grease in a Scotsman's arteries. In the winter the only escape is incest, and the insistent call of the bong.

JAMES

A DAY IN BATH

Open-top, double-decker tour buses go past my bedroom window, waking me up every morning. Hordes of grinning photographers stare in on my life.

'Fuck off,' I say, shaking my fist angrily.

'Hello,' they mouth back. 'Click-click. Thank you.'

They wave happily as I throw the contents of my ashtray at them.

In the afternoons I'm a waiter in a bistro. The women talk about how to snare rich men, the men complain because I haven't put enough '*leche*' in their '*latte*', and everybody says how 'awful' it would be to have to work for a living.

On the way home I struggle up three huge hills. And every day some silver-haired lothario nearly runs me over with his Jaguar as he tries to impress the 20-something blonde, sitting next to him, at the way he can work through the gears.

Once I was involved in an accident. The man who bumped me said it was my fault because 'only an idiot' would walk up a hill that steep. He tried to get me to pay for the damage to his Porsche as I flexed my limbs to see if they were broken. If I didn't cough-up, he said, his lawyers 'would have me eating his shit and begging for another plateful'.

When I go to bed, I can hear my neighbours screaming because Daddy's been screwing nanny. 'Well, if you put out once in a while it wouldn't happen would it dear,' says Daddy.

Soon after I fall asleep, the bus goes past and it all starts again.

ROLAND DUKE

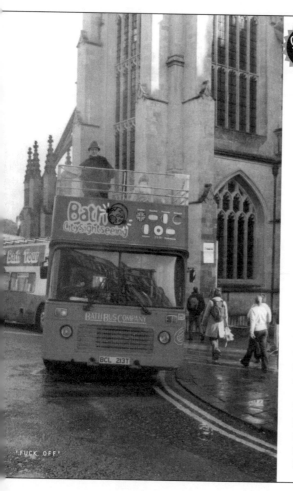

'FUCK OFF'

CRAP TOWN TRIVIA A recent survey revealed that Bath has the second worst levels of pollution from cars in the country (after Oxford, just before Glasgow). Levels of oxides of nitrogen averaged 156 parts per billion, meaning a day spent on the streets of Bath is equivalent to smoking 46 cigarettes.

AUTOGEDDON

It's clear that Bath wasn't built with the automobile in mind, but that doesn't stop the daily influx of vehicles, ranging in size from large to massive, rat-running along residential streets at breakneck speed, endangering the lives of the locals and ultimately forcing everyone to drive everywhere, in ever bigger cars, just for safety's sake.

But where are they going? Well, put it this way – the city's businesses run on the assumption that simply being in Bath is the most important thing. Details like 'having a business

plan' are low on the list of priorities, way below 'exploiting employees' and 'having a nice big company car'.

NEIL

TALK OF THE TOWN

There are two lines of conversation in Bath. Either 'Good God! You're not on the property ladder?', or 'Nerk, that smack was like wow, erm, did you know I used to be in a band?'

Except for braying Oxford-reject identikit students turtle-necking around the All Bar Ones with rugby collars poking above their v-necks, everyone is a spoilt posh kid who smokes pot.

Bath is also the only corridor-shaped place outside of the London underground where people expect you to apologise when they bump into you.

On the bright side, the buildings are nice.

DANIEL DAWKINS

CRAP TOWN TRIVIA

Bath has no fewer than four dried-flower shops.

[BAD COUNCIL]

The Roman spas in Bath have not been functioning since 1978, when they were closed on health grounds. In 2000, a £23 million project was launched to restore the historic buildings and make a new leisure complex based around the town's natural spring waters. Work was stalled when the 'wrong kind of paint' was applied to many of the structures and contractors refused to remove it.

A concert featuring The Three Tenors was held in August 2003 to celebrate the re-opening of the Spa. But it was still closed. And cobbles that were laid outside the spa building in a rush before the concert were laid incorrectly. Three weeks after being put down, they were torn up again. Costs were rocketing past the £26 million mark and, nine months later, the complex still had not opened.

GOLDEN SHOWERS

The problem with Bath isn't that it's a morose grot-hole like Grimsby or Plymouth, but that it's plain boring. Tourists love it, of course, but tourists only have to spend a day there. It's at night we really suffer. The clubs are terrible. (Consider what was until recently one of the main venues in the town, the aptly named Swamp. It had steps up to the toilet. By midnight, there was so much urine on the floor that it used to come down these stairs like a golden waterfall.) The few decent pubs are full of aggressively singing public school fools, and the walk home is blighted by 1970s buildings that look like they've been designed according to how many metal strips the council could get on the cheap from Homebase.

TIM

IN DEFENCE OF BATH

Bath is a beautiful city among rolling hills in a part of the country that enjoys a mild climate most of the year.

The large variety of individual pubs and bars are frequented by student, local, tourist and rugby fan alike – all in good harmony enjoying the pleasant surroundings that they find themselves in. If you are to get blasted, then where better place to do it than in a pub among some of the finest architecture in the country?

Pulteney Bridge and Weir, the cathedral, Pump Room, Roman Baths, the list of places to visit is absolutely huge.

Sure, Bath is expensive but you have to pay for quality. We wouldn't want it any other way. If you want a cheap city then get going, go to a poorer quality one in the North somewhere ...

JAMES W

CLAPHAM

Population: **16,000**
Unemployment: **4.7%**
Violent crime: **29 (per 1,000 per annum)**
Famous residents:
Paula Yates, Vivien Westwood, William Wilberforce (Hull born anti-slavery hero)

Of course, Clapham isn't really a town. It isn't even a London Borough (it's part of Lambeth). It is, however, resplendently awful, and that's why it's included here.

Greedheads, bimbos and braying Oxbridge rejects parade around wooden-floored chain bars in between their tedious shifts as trainee accountants or solicitors somewhere in the city.

They rent cupboards (sorry, 'designer studios') in grim, narrow streets of identical terrace houses that would be regarded as slums in the North of England, and at prices that would make the sun go pale.

Every so often you can glimpse a bleak bit of the Common, or a kebab shop selling carved up elephant legs to the Claphamites when they return home drunk from their exclusive 'watering-holes' in the West End.

Meanwhile, the old locals resent the incomers and resort to ugly violence to set the record straight. But Nathan and Sophie aren't perturbed, and anyway, the Tapas is 'just so good here'.

And so, like all the worst diseases, Clapham is spreading. Nearby Balham and Tooting are already displaying the symptoms of creative facial hair and panda-eyes from skiing. The gun-crazy residents of Stockwell are putting up a pretty strong resistance, but I'm sure it's only a matter of time before you'll have to mortgage your house before you can afford a cup of water there too.

ELEANOR ABRAMSON

COOL IT

It's not particularly original or difficult to insult Clapham. Lots of people, mainly living in Brixton, or Shepherd's Bush, sneer at its lack of 'authenticity', its glut of young white urban professionals and their attendant chi-chi boutiques.

But I like the cosseted feel of Clapham (at least the safe bits), the cafés where you get great brunches, and the interesting shops. I've even stopped getting narked at the army of joggers in their college sports kit. And how can I complain at the surfeit of young white professionals? I went to college with half of them. But what I can't cope with is the way you have to try to give the impression that you live in a carefree, entirely natural, domestic mode, while at the same time contriving to look as cool as possible. It means you can't consider even the most basic of daily tasks without being reduced to a nervous wreck.

Going to Sainsbury's has become a nightmare. Girls waft around, wearing grubby comfort clothes – comfort clothes that are never too grubby though, and never unfashionable. Tracksuit bottoms, as I understand them, should have holes in, be flecked with paint and have

elasticated ankles. They shouldn't be designed to show off your gym-toned arse. If you are so unfussed about how you are seen out, then why are you so concerned to hide VPL with a tiny pair of knickers? I'm no expert, but surely those are not comfort pants.

I'm driven insane by the types who tumble into one of the many cafés, clutching the Sunday papers and an artful ruffled look, the chap (touch rugby to play later) a little unshaven perhaps, the girl with tousled hair held in place by sunglasses, tousled hair that still manages, somehow, to be remarkably obedient.

Heaven forbid that you, like I first did, take this at face value and think that people really do wander around Clapham in precisely the same state they woke up in. I stumbled into a café on the Common, hair plastered to one side of my head and last night's gravy staining my crotch, only to discover that I was being cackled at from behind the *Style* section of the *Sunday Times*.

IAN GINSBERG

GLASGOW
Let Glasgow flourish

Population:
630,000
Unemployment: **5%**
Violent crime: **18**
(per 1,000 per annum)

% achieving achieving Scottish exam level 2 or above: **38**

Famous residents: **Darius Danesh, Lulu, Lorraine Kelly, Billy Connolly**

EDINBURGH
Except the Lord in vain

Population:
430,000
Unemployment: **3%**
Violent crime: **8**
(per 1,000 per annum)

% achieving achieving Scottish exam level 2 or above: **57**

Famous residents: **'The Proclaimers', Irvine Welsh, Gail Porter**

Mutually dependent, but locked in mutual loathing, Edinburgh and Glasgow are the conjoined twins of Scotland's central belt. While each affects to despise the other, they take a degree of interest in the goings on at the other end of the M8 which is every bit as obsessive and parochial as that of the suburban curtain-twitcher. It's no coincidence that they finished equal in the Crap Towns' rankings – just about every correspondent from Glasgow mentioned Edinburgh and every 'Burgher' had a go at the 'Weegies', neatly evening up the scores while guaranteeing mutually assured destruction.*

* Actually, one did do slightly better than the other, but we'd hate to start a civil war by revealing the true outcome.

GLASGOW

EDINBURGH

Like schoolchildren in love, they talk about each other constantly, and are not above pulling each other's hair for attention. Ask Glaswegians about this love/hate dialectic, and they will be ready to outline their grievances for the price of a can of Special Brew and a couple of Lambert & Butler. They might warm up by telling you that Edinburgh is an insufferably smug, small town with an overly keen sense of its own importance, and moreover, that it is overrun by lawyers, financiers and politicians dressed in laughable period costume (tweed!) straight off the pages of an Evelyn Waugh novel. They will tell you that Edinburgh has no decent shops and no sense of identity, having been colonised by the

EDINBURGH

English (spit). They might then proceed to state an opinion that Edinburgh people are superior, unwelcoming towards strangers and have a tendency to be somewhat too straight-laced to make for entirely agreeable company.

Alternatively, they might simply inform you that you are – as you have long suspected – a cunt.

Should you then, on your anthropological investigations, follow the good folk of Edinburgh on one of their occasional voyages westward (generally undertaken in order to enjoy some nightlife or to purchase the new 'modern style' of clothing), you will note a contrasting set of opinions. See them observing and disapproving of a terrifying rabble of Burberry-clad barbarians! Observe with them from a taxi window as young

GLASGOW

Glaswegians mill around ill-judged housing schemes and, fuelled by deep-fried pizza and export lager, get each other pregnant or – as a special matinee performance on Old Firm match days – kill each other with knives. You nod in agreement with these good Edinburgh people – how dreadful this place is! And how wet! And, as you speak to your typical Edinburgh sort, to your woman on the Morningside omnibus, you will conclude with her that all this sort of thing is all very well on *Taggart*, as long as it doesn't

- Glasgow has the unhealthiest population and shortest lifespans in Western Europe.
- 66% of the Glasgow population live in poverty.
- The three most deprived areas in the United Kingdom are in Glasgow according to a recent report by the Child Poverty Action Group.
- According to the Scottish Parliament, Glasgow contains more than three-quarters of the most deprived areas in Scotland.

WITH THANKS TO 'JAM TART'

come east and mess with the paintwork on our Audis or interfere with our expensively schooled daughters.

However, they will have hastily glossed over Glasgow's exemplary mercantile architecture, its beauty, its shopping, its friendliness and its sense of cool. Should you be gauche enough to mention these things, your new Edinburgh friend may even nod curtly in agreement, and sadly wonder what mischance led these riches to fall into the hands of the present generation of objectionable Clydesiders.

The distinction is bullshit, of course. Ned* culture is universal, and Edinburgh has pockets of poverty and desperation deep enough to make your eyes bleed, while Glasgow has its areas of wealth, Starbucks and delicatessens.

*see page 128

For myself, I take no part either in this bickering or in your cold, reductive research. How dare you? You tourist, you voyeur. I rise above it all. If anything, I'm amused by the squabbling. I see through it. I take a superior attitude to this parochial childishness. But I would, wouldn't I? I live in Edinburgh.

ED BLACK

DIRTY BLANKETS

Poverty and an air of desperation and hopelessness hang over Glasgow like a dirty blanket, a dark cloud – which might account for the perpetual rain.

The slogan that adorned buses in Edinburgh a number of years ago: 'Thank God Glasgow is miles away,' sums up the vast cultural divide perfectly.

AARON ALLEN

BREWERY SLOPS

Glasgow is full of open green spaces, and can be enjoyed at a calm pace on the Waverley steam boat, the world's very last ocean-going paddle steamer.

All the galleries and museums in Glasgow are, and have always been, free to enter. London has only recently caught up with this idea. There is a whole slew of good bars and clubs, as well as a good handful of shit pubs for the codger-at-heart. General entertaining is cheap; restaurants are reasonable and pleasant (when not serving the local 'diet').

If Edinburgh is the apogee of civilisation, why does it reek of brewery slops all the bloody time? And why is the castle in constant shame by having the busiest, most tackily commercialised street in the city running directly opposite? Why do they sell kilted, tartan, plastic dolls?

STUART WHYTE

GLASGOW

ART ATTACK

In Glasgow, I once found a three-year-old trying to break into my car with a screwdriver. Luckily, he couldn't actually reach the lock.

The local housing association tried to 'landscape' my area. They put in several large square metal bins full of weeds. The neds ripped out the weeds within a day or two, so instead the council filled the bins with concrete topped off with ornamental house bricks. Ah, urban art.

DAVID CAMPBELL

BUILD YOUR CRAP TOWN LEXICON

Neds (n) – *Scottish slang term for disenfranchised youths (it stands for Non-Educated Delinquents). Use circumspectly – Scottish Socialist MSP, Rosie Kane, wrote in the Big Issue for Scotland that it certainly wasn't appropriate for ministers to employ the term. She also pointed out that the youth in Scotland shouldn't be blamed for 'hanging around on street corners' because often there 'is nowhere else for them to go'.*

ATTACK

A mate of mine was beaten to a pulp by six men on the main Glasgow shopping street at 10 p.m. one evening simply for having a goatee beard.

DAUVIT ALEXANDER

ANTS

If there is a more miserable, brutal, godforsaken scar on the face of this planet than Glasgow, then the human race might as well let the ants take over now.

I can still recall the utter astonishment of the taxi driver I tipped last time I was there – he was clearly expecting to be robbed as usual.

The streets are paved with vomit, the inhabitants are as vicious as they are stupid, the weather is as vile as the architecture and the transport to civilisation (i.e. Edinburgh) goes via Inverness.

MIKE SIMPSON

IN DEFENCE OF GLASGOW

Glaswegians are bloody friendly. The city is steeped in history and dramatic vistas, the clubs contain the most up-for-it people I have ever witnessed, and some of the restaurants are the best in the UK.

EDINBURGH

In addition to this, you will never see a sunset as dramatic within the British Isles.

Give us any more crap Simpson and I will give you an honorary Glasgie kiss you SASSENACH!!!!!!
'SUE HUGHES'

SOME CORRECTIONS
Firstly, it's spelt sassanagh. Secondly, 'sassanagh' is what the highlanders called the lowland inhabitants of Scotland after the English invaded and took it over in the 600s. So, you are insulting yourself. Indeed most of the lowland 'Scots' possess English genes. And yes, Glasgow, unlike Edinburgh, is a shite hole.
UNBEATABLE LIONHEART

BUSTED
The playwright Tom Stoppard said that rather than being the Athens of the North, Edinburgh is the 'Reykjavik of the South'. Edinburgh is cold in all sorts of ways: the people, the buildings, the gaps in the cityscape caused by the hills, and especially the all-year-round icy winds.

The bus drivers are contenders for the title of the UK's most psychotic public transport employees. Only in Edinburgh have I seen a bus driver pull out in front of an elderly woman clutching a white stick with the intention of making an example of her.

ANON

DRUG DEN

In the summer, Edinburgh is a charming cosmopolitan wonderland full of opportunity, different accents and sexy Antipodean immigrants.

After mid-September it turns into a freezing seething drug den cleaved through with running rivers of pissed-up students. People will only talk to you at Christmas, and then only shoplifters trying to flog Superdrug perfume 'for yer missus'.

J. IRELAND

ROVING REPORTER'S VERDICT

DEEP-FRIED MARS BARS. They aren't an urban myth: they are available in both Glasgow and Edinburgh. I ate one on a cold December night. It was quite nice. Then I was sick.

SJ

3

SUNDERLAND
Nil desperandum auspice deo
(Don't worry, trust God)

Population: **280,00**
Unemployment: **5%**
Violent crime: **10.6 (per 1,000 per annum)**
% achieving 5 or more GCSE grades A–C: **42**
Famous residents: **Alf Wight (aka James Herriot, the vet), Kate Adie, Dave Stewart (guitarist with beard)**

Sunderland was the biggest ship-building port in the world until it was bombed to smithereens in World War II. Now it's more famous for being the biggest city in Europe without a cinema, and one of the BNP's favourite stomping grounds.

Not so much a town as a mortuary. Industry has long departed, leaving the residents to shuffle around the town's meagre consumer options like zombies in a George A. Romero movie – while seagulls shit on them.

DANIEL ETHERINGTON

'SOUTHERN BASTARDS, FUCK OFF'

The Crowtree Leisure Centre dominates the centre of this town. Rusting and stained with grime, and the ever-present bird poo, it is divided by a walkway where old men gather to gawp through the glass at swimming children.

There's graffiti at the bus station reading 'Southern bastards – fuck off back south and keep the North East Northern' in 3 feet high lettering.

I also had a landlord who once told me: 'We don't like outsiders, us. A lot of people want that university closed.'

SHAUN ALCOCK

STREET OF SHAME

I used to live on Amberley Street – as featured on *Crime Watch* and *Panorama*'s special on car crime. Pretty cool if you wanted weed and violence off the Hell's Angels chapter who used to live in a bricked-up house. I say, 'used to live' because the council decided in its wisdom to knock down the whole street. I suppose, at least, there won't be any more managers of the Tap and Spile tied up and held at

gunpoint in the cellar with the phone lines cut so that the locals can deal drugs from the front bar as if it were Wendy Herbal Supermarket.

Sunderland's local girls (wifeys) are very skilled at applying orange foundation with the cleanest tidemark I've ever seen – so in line with the cheek that their pasty necks can still proudly show the litter of trophy love bites. While I used to wear long-Johns, jeans, two T-shirts, a jumper, two jackets and a hat in the winter, the locals wear very cheap, light cotton summer clothes with packs of Royal 25s neatly placed up their T-shirt sleeves.

ANON

SOFA SO BAD

One night when I worked in Sunderland, I made the mistake of staying at a colleague's house in the notorious Pennywell area of the town and as we were walking down the bank to his house at 3 a.m. we were overtaken by a burning sofa.

KEITH WHALEN

MORONS

You morons!

Ever been to Seaburn or Roker, you useless twats? Come and see me and I'll tell you all about Sunderland while I'm stoving your head off a pavement.

ANDY HUNNS

IN DEFENCE OF SUNDERLAND

It's easy to sneer. Sunderland is not without its problems, but we've come a long way after the years of blight which followed the collapse of our shipyards and the entire Durham coalfield. Unemployment is lower than at any time during the last 30 years. The magnificent Stadium of Light has risen from the ashes of the former Wearmouth pit (the quality of the football varies, though at the time of writing we are on the up). The university is flourishing. Our riverside has been transformed. There is excellent public transport. Anyone on a national pay scale – teacher, nurse, public officer – has a far higher disposable income than their equivalent further south because of the relatively cheap housing. My wife (who is Vietnamese) and I (one of those allegedly despised Southerners) have lived happily near the city centre – not far from Amberley Street – for 17 years without experiencing any of the prejudice and bigotry to which your correspondents refer. I don't deny that it may sometimes exist. *But*, the impression given by your informants paints a picture that is grossly distorted.

CHRIS MULLIN, MP

[BAD COUNCIL]

A point of local controversy is the Seaburn fountain. This is located on a traffic island in a coastal suburb of the city, coincidentally where artistic miserabilist L.S. Lowry used to go for holidays in the 1960s, and where some claim Lewis Carroll was inspired to write *The Walrus and the Carpenter* (a local myth, I'm afraid). One of a number of public artworks commissioned by the council, this squat concrete structure was controversial from the outset.

Built at a cost of £200,000 in 1989, it was slammed at the time as 'money down the drain' by 86% of residents and is regularly slated in the letters column of the *Sunderland Echo*. Touted by the council in 1989 as one of the 'world's most spectacular fountains', it no longer emits jets of water and instead a profusion of weeds are growing from the top of it. Councillors now say that the fountain, built in part with European funding, could not be demolished without a slice of the money being repaid to the EU.   JOE SWAN

WINDSOR
In unitate felicitas
(You're better off in a union)

Population: **28,000**
Unemployment: **2%**
Violent crime: **8.3**
(per 1,000 per
annum)
% achieving 5 or
more GCSE grades A-C: **71**
Famous residents: **HM
Queen Elizabeth II, Elton
John, numerous small dogs**

*The royal family liked Windsor so
much that they named
themselves after it. Lesser
mortals may enjoy its beauties,
but can't help feeling ripped-off.*

The big thing about Windsor is that its townsfolk believe that by living near the castle they are more-or-less royalty themselves. Indeed, once Windsor women pass the age of 60, they seem to lose the plot altogether and convince themselves that they actually are the Queen. You can often spot these old dears in the town centre, sporting HRH-style hair-do's and spectacles and waddling as regally as they can, with their handbags draped daintily over their wrists.

Windsor has its moments of joy. On a wintry Saturday night, a meal and a walk in the town centre can be little short of idyllic. But for each of these instants, Windsor has hours of hell. In the summer, the tourists invade and you can't even get to the shops to buy milk on a hung-over Sunday morning without fighting through hordes of smiling fools wearing Manchester United replica shirts and taking photographs of lamp posts and litter bins. Even the swans get cheesed off and sneer menacingly at any that come too close to them.

The castle is spectacular, and it's all a few minutes stroll away from quaint old Eton. But this charm is compromised by the presence directly outside the castle of nearly every fast food chain you can think of: Starbucks, McDonalds, Burger King, Pizza Hut.

The local fudge shop sucks too, with its female hawkers who stand outside the shop dressed up in ridiculous costumes shrieking: 'Do you want free fudge?' in improbably high-pitched voices at disinterested, embarrassed passers-by. (Memo to

these women: No, we don't.)

There was recently a campaign to replace the 'SL' part of the Windsor postcode to disassociate the area from nearby Slough. I know who these people are. They're the ones who, when asked where they live, will always say: 'Oh, in Windsor... near the Queen!' (even though she's hardly ever in town); they will never say: 'In Windsor, near Slough' (even though that's geographically correct).

CHAS NEWKEY-BURDEN

WINDSOR PHOTOS: SAM JORDISON

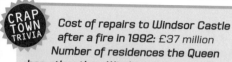

CRAP TOWN TRIVIA

Cost of repairs to Windsor Castle after a fire in 1992: £37 million

Number of residences the Queen has other than Windsor: 7

Annual amount taxpayers contribute to maintenance of the Queen's houses: £16 million (approx.)

Cost of maintenance of Windsor Castle: not available

Annual cost to taxpayers for Queen to travel between her houses: £18 million

Annual electricity bill for the Queen: £326,000

Annual gas bill for the Queen: £334,000

Cost of Queen's porters and cleaners: £500,000

Annual cost to taxpayers to house non-royal unemployed mother of four: £7,000

When is the Queen resident at Windsor Castle? Some of April

WINDSOR CASTLE: QUEEN HAS NO PLANS TO MOVE

LUTON

1

Population: **184,000**
Unemployment: **4%**
Violent crime: **12.2**
(per 1,000 per
annum)
% achieving 5 or
more GCSE grades A-C: **43**
Famous residents: **Paul**
Young, John Hegley (poet),
Boddingtons Beer (really,
look on the can), Lorraine
Chase once sang a song
about the airport

Too close to London to warrant
building anything approaching
what the capital has to offer, yet
just far enough to away to offer a
sense of other-worldly, neglected
isolation, Luton had to be top of
the list.

"ARE YOU STUCK HERE FOR THE DAY?"

'Only losers take the bus' is the attitude of the Lutonian. Once, having waited for 50 minutes in the town centre for a bus to take me home along one of the four different routes I can use, I asked the driver whether Arriva would ever deliver a decent service to the people of Luton. 'As good as they deserve,' came the answer.

JONATHAN HALL

SHITE

Luton's industry continues to die. Has taken 30 years so far and still going. Not necessarily a bad thing though. As I remain employed in one of the last remnants of the British (alright, American) car industry, my one memory of those that have left the brick and iron temple to global pollution is the constant claim 'I can't fucking wait to get out. Working here is shite.'

JAMES S

MEN-FISH

As a town built on the River Lee, the planners have made superb attempts to make this facility pertinent to the needs of the local Lutonian. Or not. It has been for the most part covered by the concrete town centre sprawl, while the exposed stagnant ditch meanders drearily by the side of the Old Bedford Road. I can only assume this is to stop any local halfwits from falling in more than an inch of this filth, and over-burdening the already stretched facilities of the Luton & Dunstable hospital with more 'men-fish'.

A fine town indeed, but sadly one I shall not be visiting any more as everyone I know has either died or moved to Raunds.

ANDREW CLIFT

STUCK

I have lived here for less than a year. When we arrived, we went to the tourist information centre. The woman asked, 'Did you have a flight

that was cancelled? Are you stuck here for the day?' She went on to say that there really wasn't any place in Luton worth visiting, but that it is close to some lovely countryside.

An elderly woman asked me,

'How are you finding Luton?'

I wanted to be diplomatic.

'Well,' I said, 'people say they tore the heart out of the town when they demolished so much of it to build the Arndale Centre.'

'It never had much of a heart,' she replied.

NAME WITHHELD

IN DEFENCE OF LUTON

Luton has everything except the sea ... but it does have sea cadets.

Yes Luton is unloved by the critics but it's

certainly lovable. It's a town that celebrates its diversity big time: in some schools over 30 languages are spoken; it celebrates slapsticks day, Mela and, of course, the biggest one-day carnival in the UK. Indeed, so good are we at celebrating that we're about to have the UK's first, and only, National Carnival centre located here. And if you need a break from the hurly burly of the town centre, how about the Downs surrounding the town, the historic Luton Hoo or a trip from Luton airport to a million and one exotic locations?

MARGARET MORAN, MP

INDEX